Thief of Hearts

Thief of Hearts

Maxwell Owen Clark

ROOF BOOKS
NEW YORK

ISBN: 978-1-7379703-1-6
Library of Congress Control Number: 2021952805

NEW YORK | Council on This book is made possible by the New York State
the Arts Council on the Arts with the support of the Office of
the Governor and the New York State Legislature. .

Roof Books
are published by
Segue Foundation
300 Bowery, New York, NY 10012
seguefoundation.com

Roof Books
are distributed by
Small Press Distribution
1341 Seventh Street
Berkeley, CA. 94710-1403
800-869-7553 or spdbooks.org

"The plot of proximity and communication is not a modality of cognition. [...] It is not due to the contents that are inscribed in the said and transmitted to the interpretation and decoding done by the other. It is in the risky uncovering of oneself, in sincerity, the breaking up of inwardness and the abandon of all shelter, exposure to traumas, vulnerability."

—E. Levinas, *Otherwise than Being* (III., 5-6)

"And Anarchy, the Skeleton,
Bowed and grinned to every one,
As well as if his education
Had cost ten millions to the nation."

—P. B. Shelley, *The Mask of Anarchy*

Power Move

Left Right
Right Left
Up Down B.

Bucolic irradiationsStain
bluish dungInto facial
creases.Obsidian sparkling
dungWells upOver
furrows.Animated by
efflusion of the sund,isis ae
trae of its excess.But allo
this must be erased, in

order tO sub-tain "the" proper moenumtin of thoht. The uthoragon must rEMember to fO.rget,nod,to exdpend witout reserve. Tremor with echoesOpening the flehsT.o us les e ejaulatio.ns.Cup skull and buttks,pıft of luxurit efflu.

.. ..
.......hushhhhhhhTgrilling, tdrilling disclosureOffephwe obsidian swarmsFrom antennae lush.Oop! an.nise-rep.rodution.Hy.pérphy.sical deli.veran.ce
graing.s Ric.rdo. Peeing there the shite, hisd jutting forth as a brace urns its reteeming.oo —Weak turbulence-patter.ning of grasses touched by winds. Lips gluing up SWOOning cusps. A culling of aroundness. *Vents of eroticism fan out ALONG ossatures of feeling.* AN covenal. i. Prishmatic razlors gute his dodility. Dobistep grimi coruscates bastslings |m|o|m|nipotent. Silk-coated hyenas ignite corporeally. Altis alw alr ant imm recyclg.
^^^^^^^^^^^^^^^^^^

1o

Arriva. t gorgons grasp.ing all.A p.ening. ^of 6789 this regionaLity.

GuiLtiest convolutions wended along. <u>Latencies</u> recoiled in immanence. A thousand invisible threads tie Micaracardo's heart to the

\\\\\\\\\\\\\\\\\\\\\\""""""""".............. ...."""""""""""""""""""""""""///// ,,,,,,,,,,,,,,,,,,,,,,,

masseres. Exhaustion

s ove im. ullen, ditid snow as raiments for the clearing. Bicardo's zpores heave with anguish. He is

•▼•

.. ....

{op_{ened unto yet}   )

(inconstruablepla   }

{||/..

c s. Coconcommunion pours through t.
   A n z asphalt paaking lot dappled
with geoluminescent facets swims

bes id e the soccer field.

Counterings _____

_____ juxtapose

at all his ************ **** ** ******* * * .. ,,******   interstices.

A   consolidating

unshelters all thisity._____ R-

_e-_c__o— - i-l. s torque the brittle
weave of ^^^^^^^. ^^^^^. ^^^^^^^[∴]
^ ^

externappality. It is done. Clutterings
plate scales over-upon his fleshy lenses. Money eases the
friction of hermeneutic distance.

=======+========== = =+ =.   += = == = =\\|| |. |]

[A♠...
♠
♥]

                                        floodlight.

_____;::_____|/_____

____−_-

_____   __.   __'   '_____ _−__ __−−

_////////////]##

gOliceanic maws consume him again. An ..,., ' '
"..,. . .odiferous copse of arbors .   .,. —*_-.,semi-
circumscribe ...,,..-,—\. #. . .   **   .. .# [⊡] .. ;;;
_;;;;;;, ,.., ,.his flank. . T h e smearing retains phenomenal
traces of Ricardo's care packages. She is undesealable.

Her |o e [⊡] |\| gg

<>i<>i<>

i

s' \

given over

to.

~ ` ` /'<.

● Agully offerns undu

lates   eneath loodlights. Neocolonial architectures

unfurl peripherally. Night enwombs around Yicardo a
murex

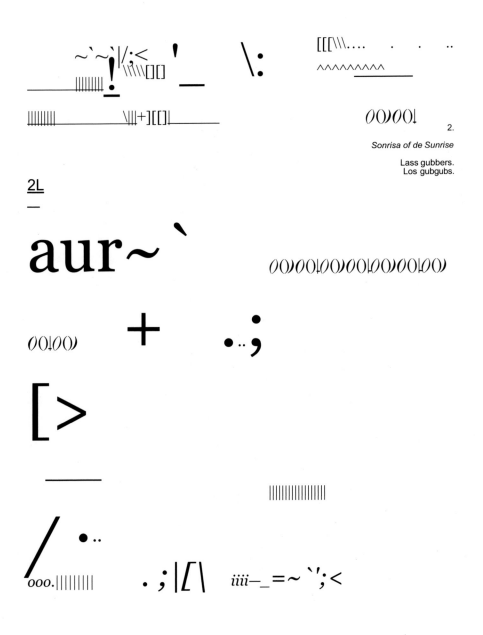

Sonrisa of de Sunrise

Lass gubbers.
Los gubgubs.

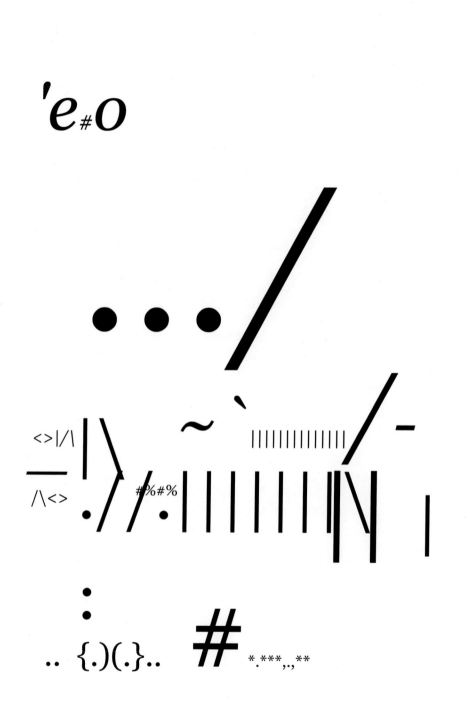

/////

-_-

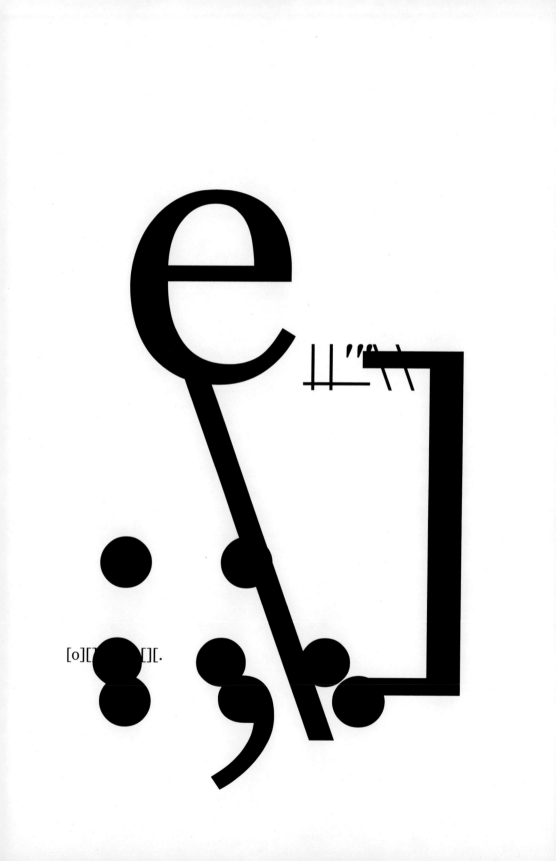

He p**u**lls on at^ta yoy-w*oy!* '—'=|—doit iyoint **de**murely. Hish peetLing-there-unto-aze circleates withub thwe tissuesesisi of d**e** frummwe L.a.los.ao Thingus-Loierd||. He im^agines being an

ally rap

====^==

ed. uz3*   (((itibitilitlpriti))) Dungk-golden darkiness in the **cre||as|es\||.** of imperialistiaq biolenceiaj, tremborl;ing bhis pissisibÆnessTewq aspb abp bhellbeau. REALLY UNFREAL "The" streets are

up welling, >>>

@....   **,l'Àɫ**

he**a**ving, , ,,   ,   , ,

< <gee

W I. L. L. I. C. K. E. R.   S 'q^>> **<   <**

<<

nnnnnnnnnn..............'.......... ··.'..............

·.'·...   **STARRY**

＊

＊＊＊

+

                star_star**Ǐ＊**＊＊.   ＊   star

  ＊   ＊   ＊ 88 8star

   starstar.   .|| . +++   ＊   ＊

————————s—L—o—o—P—s—i^＊ —————————＊   —————

_____——_\.

)O\|{[__=|\>.;|||||

S

Rheicador trace a/a n^{e}c^{r}o^{p}o^{l}i^{t}i^{c}a^l cirkle — a b. s.   e.

n.   t. *O( )}{* circumference or center. unmarked terrain of unmarked subsoil sunken skulls gaze through his gaze. I want to someday stop all hurting people with my words.All becomes glommed with spit. *World-trauma screepsin.*M i k i a r d o i s b l a n k e t e d b y t h e t r i l l i n g o f a m b i e n t e c h n a g g l u t i n a t i v e a .   **Arachnitisi** swarm out of his father's rent breast • Apertures dilate ● Interfaces become poor us ●   A blik constellation swarm of secrecies escends. Flikardo   metamorphoses   into   a   D<u>A</u>SH<u>IN</u>G   ==> [[[.R.H.I.L.I.Q.I.S.H.I.D.A.O.G.U.N.G.F.U.]]]

peacock-deer, then a R E S O U N D I N Gg-'\,; - - - -   __.

—

                             • • •#@##

\\

,

- resounging tortoise].
OoUuRrRrEe   ]][ ]\\\\|||||||\\\\|//////[/\\\\
    ⊿⊔⊔|?\\\\||||||||\\\\\\|//////\\\\⊔|||?//\V////\V////\\\\||||||\\\\|/
//\\\\\V||||?   //\V/////   • •
[•//////\\\\||||||\\\\|//////\\\\⊿⊔⊔|?//\V/////\V/////\V////\V////

        //

              mbs \\\\\\|

||||| | | \\•• \\\\\\|/ _____ - -__. _
  — —   //••/ --__._---
                  //\
                      • • • •\• •

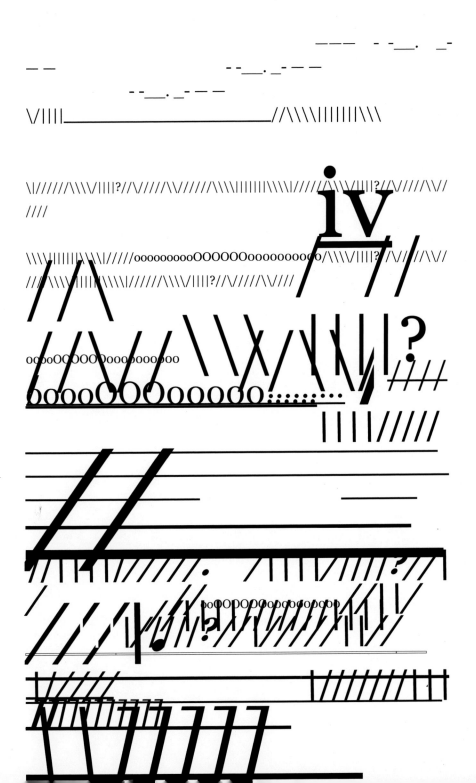

// __ //]]]][.

[[[[[[[·]

6-0-987-_
/
789

35=/=45
13-0-

oOo the sate of oOo   the
oOoOoOOooOoooOo

-D-A-S-H-I-N-G-

_R_E_S_O_U_N_D_I_N_G_

soccer field

Riardi

name

hithot

n_um_er rbs.

Everything
bestles
within a

.h_{est}li_{ng} ●

PLURReffe._____
_____ ni—

plurredeniomagdartawaz
e ···················...Usherd .
isolation is flingked with
an/ `z //. nise.;' eLSRWSe
eckommuni°n. ;' `~~/
Whickardo . collesks
sarhds orf osamic.
'e ‥ ►⊏

n
⊩⊪⊪⊪⊩

. * * *

doe th-

ing withou en, r nds -- freeomn s n effluz f th ueles, ucessary.|

U|.n.e.v||.e.n./~.';-<= 18^p=<-- X~.'; bt

~~omkbined isect weqwosonances pendis-~~
~~eclosrd ithin i i te ull f ernbs. leyocardo hs~~
~~orgottenfph smuuch sin~~cshe

]]]]]]]]]]]]]]][[[[[[[[[[[[[[[[[[[[[]]]]]]]]]]]]]]\\\\\\\\\\\\\\\\\\\\\[[[[[]]]]]}{}
{}{}{}

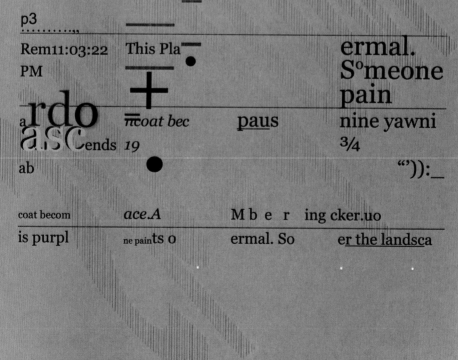

p3 ··········,,

Rem11:03:22 PM	This Pla	ermal.
		S°meone pain
rdo asCends 19	πcoat bec	nine yawni
a	paus	3/4
ab		")):__

| coat becom | ace.A | M b e r ing cker.uo |
| is purpl | ne paints o | ermal. So er the landsca |

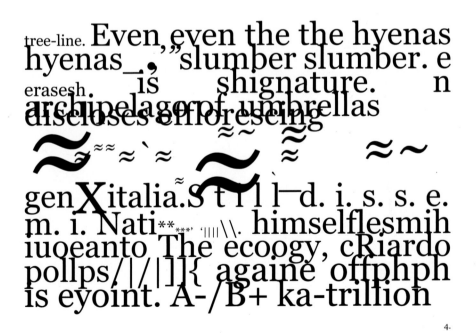

tree-line. Even, even the the hyenas
hyenas_, "slumber slumber. e
erasesh. is shignature. n
archipelagoof umbrellas
discloses efflorescing

≈ ≈ ≈ ≈ ` ≈ ≈ ≈ ≈ ~

genXitalia. S t i l l─d. i. s. s. e.
m. i. Nati**₊***' '||||\\. himselflesmih
iuoeanto The ecoogy, cRiardo
pollps/|/|]{ againe offphph
is eyoint. A-/B+ ka-trillion

bor**************** mmoore
selveffsagesidades##.———~
——— Ḧ.ave circleaort.ed
throu.gp.. h ..iss.p frnam.e.
Hiso so.ereintii ripple.soo in
subatomic · orbits.eaoi
belkcomes fihx.kated ino at
llya.ndscape -- inshoo "The"
optic memorimentoesa of a
near-distant satellite.

Chrematistics articulate th. Socaile

organs of sensuousness

onunicoagulate. Lushdness wells up in in up in himsh.

Incomprehens.

ible

detours..

$\overline{b}$ t r a y the

(e|\\|sored. Trees

like   entombed nymphs.

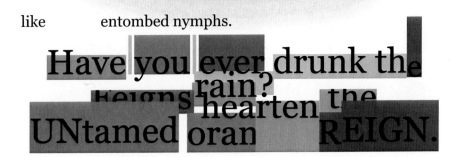

Have you ever drunk the rain? reigns hearten the UNtamed oran REIGN.

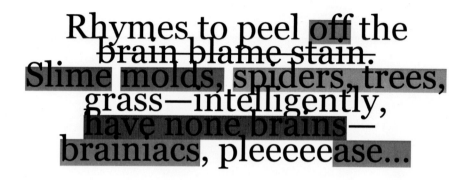

Rhymes to peel off the
brain blame stain.
Slime molds, spiders, trees,
grass—intelligently,
have none brains—
brainiacs, pleeeeease...

. =

Diademed.   ---
    ma.sturbati.on. Our
dictates field mouse satte.
dictates   of his taste.
                              NE
>< O BEEP   TWIET
MEAR
DENDRE WOBE HS
WAUT><.L.   e.   a. v.
e s   of   the   gullyAll   with
go.L den rb ulen ce
veinsT,uib e r-o pt c
hrown.
tyoke th ings mor e   tightly
decapitated.The e Decoupled   d
ferns brea hes mullintply.
species   . com bust   on

geoLogical time-

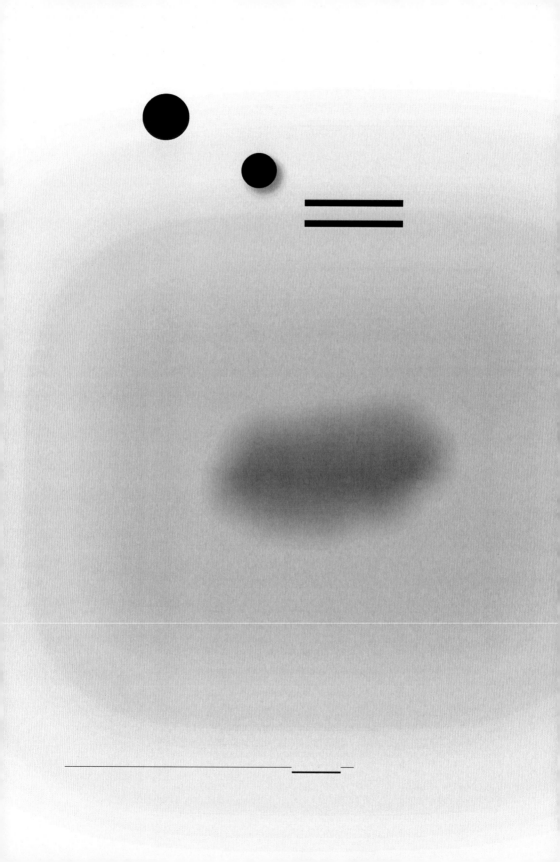

subjectivities.,, subjectalentamentotenativities verything nospires degether. He is a strickenate, a

begriev'dt, ₕearthstorn, tet maLto re_funa.gee o_f aLL puntsticks and "‚‚" í́

Ẅ ņ ǎ

ᶠL_ES^H F_LE^SH _FL^ES_H is FL_o̊o̊DSPed wover whyth paucities and mediocrities.

ₜhe feeld disjoi LLntsLLL{} []LLLL|LLLL.[] .

.

LLLa_La LL˴/_LLLLLLL. .LL-;'` ~|ᴸLLLL\

LLLL^LLLL-*.,&*‡̄`~|;"., o Lissing archmeant The_

Lissing   The

archmeant

`L L L L. L L . . . . L L L L L L L

L L.LLLL . L L .L L``

`L L.
L and joints in copulation with him.
Catègorĭcał ғʟeshpotery, well, ŏver. Ħe smothers the end of the joint against a stone and then chucks it into the surrounding woods.For allSuch thatThere existsFor allThere exists.Torrents of jubilation seize his whirling complexus. archotic beatificatio n smoothves hiv hair. jInky

ilk vortiques coagulaterre. Ba   ccha'na n-habitings jowl

puzzy   andrs
                · Riri's   h   diemble buds of

z'cannabie ino an envelope of ERFEC

bowlling plaper.

J ust So wIth p turn out anothre eyoint. Him plands

pift itte To his mouth just suur, ark hs g'hter aft a fewf gooshles, theneht he inpales sooftly. Te ollo splane f te skoccer feeld-rng s October-imming. Cardo«==extrapolates==»intercorporealities«==. Feudal rabbit-warrens wilt recrudescent. Frothing intercourse.Supersaturated with poodliness. Chream ast locokracy. Mediocre gobblinn. Un-eversal torture. Squawking. Astronomic songs branded upon the heart.

56
``` ``````` ```` ````,,,, , ,, >==============o8--+

Hypor-batucada triumphantaline "in" "the" burn turn. U-nirsal unicoossive trauba. XPXhXaXrXmXaXcXoXlXoXgXy Externa©M. O. C. | acceleraand immandecai neua ozoluiton. esubective laor ff naual apopiation.hainsaws gu Rirdo's testicles. Hss allow omb'd x pulates a dressive pisode. Hyppolyrhymic ivison ot abor.urningtrings eethe vious. Haps diyrab ntalgic.Songs sung singingly. Visher- weasels prey upon rassic nostriches. Picardo is Phicardo inna aother.---cubator poms. Numinous insights dissolute. Remodeling.
```

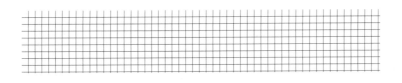

Digi-claps Tiggered.pers'delight.Poesivipostohes. Utimately fuile luxr of alltita pbeeing. Tublar nariness. *Decrescendos* of om ni poten ce. Velveteen moss populates his touch. Petrified barbs rake against his turbulence. All is nesting ab fungi. His yloint giftbags enspiraled libations of incense to her clearing under 3am black fur hood. Exhaustive circumlocutions. Every otprint an ahive. Tim accretes as does the ATHEMATICALI spiral of a snail shell. Aardo tastes sooty blueberries. Glacial wounds melt tears into the dung-blue creases of his raccoon-face. Uneven

ut combined liber- ation extant even in mic`rologies. echnology more human

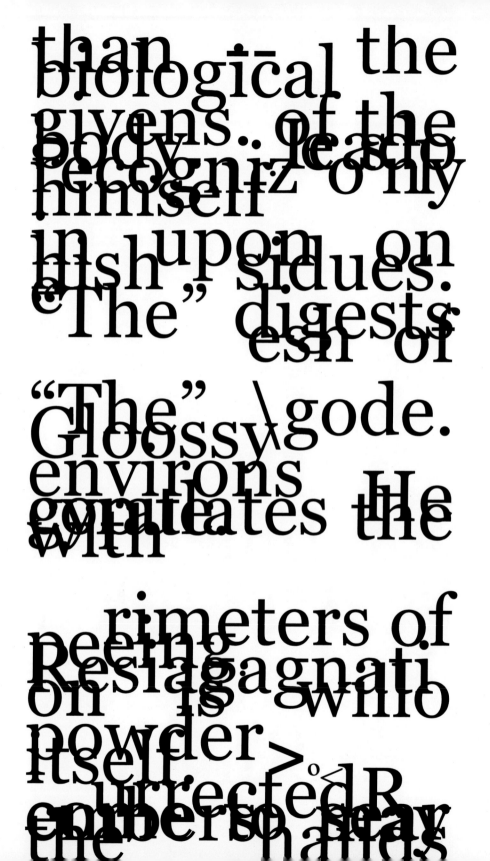

attended

at once

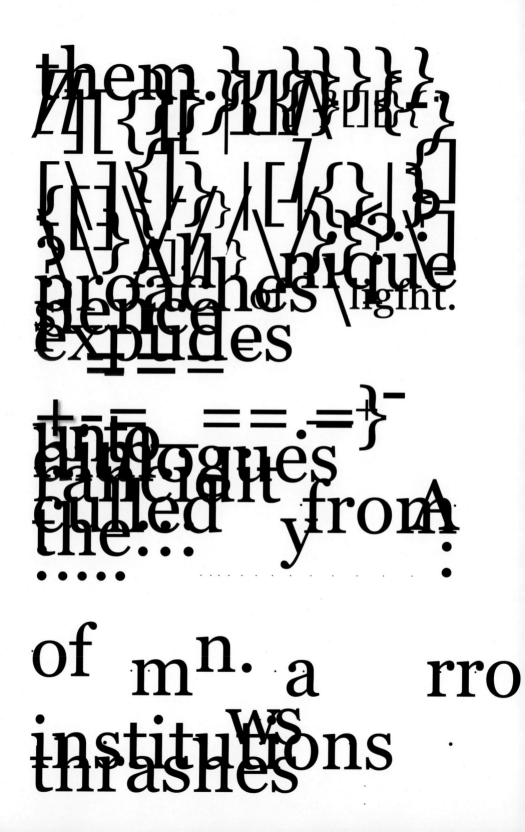

within him.

All
itosis   acnes

with
Aecoming.
i 'thisnes
encrusted
mportant.··· e
aends   the
oimpaction o
f e   wold ith as •
$|_|PERN|ATTURAL Hi velationsRe.

IIs Isuousness ermineates lls Jassing moteness. T soccer fEeld feelding him is a monstmocty.inter's waw s ver ollapsing ocver hm. Miutely comressed-coressing digaiali. Hypbuance of vetor calulaions

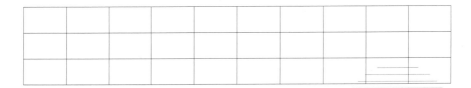

. As the returning/ spiral dadvances. Lon waterg-gassres
de efined   he   wnd.

Rorodynam c
bingle   leaf.
dying   leaf.

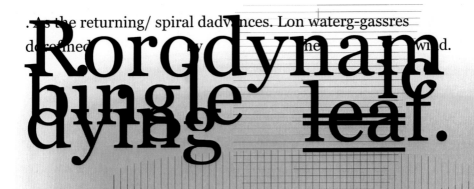

Untranslatable f||o e precipitates in the snield. A river of fire
pours through. Bodly artic l ti s fined t ch ologically.
Unwns filtered

```
x
 xx
  xxx        ><
   xxxx
    xxxxx
     xxxxxx
```

"I am as tall as these mountains. I run the field."

"Yeah, yeah. You don't even know how you hurt me."

"I am the them, they would be we, y'all."

"Tell them the naked male consort of Jesus in the bible story."

"It said he had a most beloved disciple too."

"Max!"

"Yes?"

"Will you please stop this."

. .. .
. ...

7

diagonally. and dances.Communicididerationalismus. Halibut acids age hotel deshplots.inja vesus muraisa.An dexcessive blift dof ar p^ook. A disganizatio nverng tords tot;l. 8-:x. Rido smurns hissah plown pur e anquished illionbs. Haoniums throom alog t stradn. Ceerested macinaions graze ostrich-like. Muirimiurs coinitiniue wealalaing uapa. Gootted spinnards offal a coherent conceptual armature. Hollows and warrens seething emblems. Knuckled ridges. Iridescent rings telescope. Scalped craniums jut out in obscure patterns.

Volepshtuous etaters toured.Satanic shame manifests. Paid into depression.Trunkvercation. YArrhythmia. Peentension abounding, ineborable. Violent outcomes indicated microscopically. Nebulishmettes orbit noids. We are extravagantly placed along the suburban golf course.

Dilated jaguars poont prails of their own being behind them.

#////#///JJJJJ]]]]]////p... ... .

Ardoc cocoons himself. Numerous self-redactions blessedly cripple this plessherd xt. Ubumdled mutilicities sorge thog it is meshwork. Fishles stid Rird's sept. Mumued puteseces of brifiancieres ix the felding WHOOPORWHORLWhirling utake of nevou timuli
The Metaphysics of Reading: "Nothing".

8

overdownupwhelming. Neo-beon-zurest lichen. Thees NEU order of things dizes. He quashles his whipples.acramental hots of labor-value shepherd us along. Ded, feund leaes poulate his nosrils. Silent, entless, inanible, asteless immility of the imossile. Neation goopls itself up in the interstices.Weafve umbers into this hingt-magkin, bubehomlle, proel it into an ovewelingr exetionre,Exhaust it unto death,Such chremastic energy sinksAlso secrete an efflux of freedom.Profane hallucinations wax largeAnd tall grass-whorls rush patterned --Clouds fractalize along their perimetersWorld nervature contortedAs the returned spiral advances.

An aspiration of pheromonesWilts iridescent hollows and warrens.A touch of categorical slurringsAll along echo chambers.Individuation as creeping extinction.

asver-quep.Lilly-pad archipelagoes pixelate.Gahe hildc's faceoncaves cinto mist;---A shroud stitched around the perimeters of corporeality. Intoxicated reunion defers reification.Sad nimbi cloud the canton.Reverberations undulate along inconstruable ridges. Convections of hatred populate across The filde.

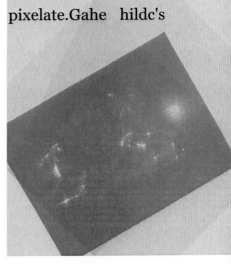

97

Fdoled within checkpoints and blast walls. Anting best, rhead.Vehiculars of inertium yecrcle fowaad.Quaking neutralities abate unto treachery.Timbral texture of a porous murmur.ahe.   DO-DI-ahe.Overtones of void-subjects Containerizing urt bobality;Dismantling mantles;acidicismic churnPolyvalent whirligigs swoon. Analogue noise-blankets coma. Flaring sepsos convolute. Paralytic deserts seethe.All is usenledaGlakial owunds melt. Truncation of peing.Rew adv. Sculpting the medial void.n-faedck.DISHPERIAL MORELADS CINJUREATE OBALLO FENESTRAtiONIt takes a lot of means to be an end-in-oneself. Bigitaialio perfumes this thing.Sorrow is harvested from yeast.Shivering euphoria of revulsion.Bucolic lawns insulated by lucre.

I. $\overline{I}$ *am the one who hears from afar.*I rinkd maté ferrousingly. Hypercathexi obliterate their substratum-mechanism. Nonnything I itewr pwyll cocombe to inter-de-un-pre-proto-relate to anything I wike. Mighty leaves vomited up by the torsion of displaced atmospheres. j*Lust dankce.* Halogen light bulbs are the new dawn. Veins crackle with paint, venom. Infidelity of this dead branch. Vacuous

10

innovations. pseudo-Ptolemaic self-as-sun. Waves of fir (I. Codelio):I am the last who would redeem you with the word. Impossible book. Impossible of books. (*the impossible happens.*)Mint odioces arette bever a zezeading wiseosum. Glorious to be in such graces as these. Carnality envelopes out an incorporealizing drive. Log drums puke puuils. Gelvis ArANcia troddidods a necroeon-pastel tace through the bantudexburbs of NYC. All teaching unlearns. Appearance-in-itself. So preciously belabored an interminable outpouring. Levis Arcgia is sober. Abodes wither and flourish. *Cupping of being into itself.* Slaps of blood remble. Triadics zoom scalar . Wanton hact . Tracts, digestsI. 'being in fact a living corpse -- the one who has been defeated and spared'Indigestion of anietxy. Atrophic dispersals. To achieve nothing new, neither anything old. Stepping back into the popening.I. Nlight sist darkl. Belvis Gharncia sleeps in hotels sometimes. Ancestral geological sedimentation of the built environment, bible tech blouses. Exoskeletal architectures. To rub embers against the grain of history.

11

Your cups outpoured,   [][][][][]
Quenched our wretched thirsts,   [][][][][][]
[][][][][] Smoothed our hair,[][][][][][][][][][][][][][][][]
[][][][][][][]Filled up our empty, alien souls,

X.XX....XXXXXXXX XXXXXXXXXXXXXXXXXXXXXXXXXXXXX
xxBestowed exquisite peace,\   \\
        \\\\\\\\

                \\\\\\\\\\\\\\\\\\\\\\\\\\\\\\\We,   who, live,,   dead,,,,   under,,,,,,,, Abomination.tion.tion.tion.tion.tiooooon.I am but one face of a coinThe other of which is an atlas.Sip slowly, delikalalentale from the urn of abomunism.'The only intelligible language in which we converse with one another consists of our objects in their relation to each other.'The unformulated remainder is the (Comprehensive Grammar) gift of every text.Afford (nobby) hospitality to the clandestine,I cant wite no's blother. I transmit pure self.

bothersome passage above.Reduies phf isituional ritigs (species, race, genealogy) mrint The wentl fesh asi econd ature.Urbanity leads everywhere, coheres the topology of humankind -- the countryside is a furrowed ribcage of the city. Non, the first city was a farm.Bellow thissa shiphiste.A murmured antiphon and tatterdemalion hospitality as whispered thr**I**gh this latticework. Gorly eb ot flesyhthyself aster sockciety , raccoon-eyed, nest as spiders in our lungs.

12N, e.q.e. 'The Thing Still There When You Turn Away'

nestle in thou, lurve, as snow wreathes our hair. Leviathan-jackals caw: *Nos mar un jardín de espumas, y nos jardín un mar de flores*. Erotic libraries and amphetamine salts. Synonymic ice-jumps. Abysses of sophistication. Anti-encyclopedic reserves. Sprouting a pair of spiraled ibex antlers. Invisible gloves. Immanence, not imminence. Obsidian razors gut the empty shell of will and grace of a docile child.terminal insomnia. Cherubim piss acid. Fiber-optic yokes.'I am without kingdom,I shall reign, I reign, I have reigned.'Integral disjointures. Rancorous copula.Aerial photographs. The book of humanity is patterned on the theological scrolls. Obsolete scintillations. Everything becomes a model for everything else. Hollows and planes. Pro-stat-hesis de of gode. Calendrical hegemony. Stimulant grimy. Deconstructures of feeling:'If you ain't in my dollars then you ain't in my senses.'If only to forget were as easy as to keep silence.To be minutely precious, while maintaining a true taste for language.To give a means of social relation, a grafting in and of consciousness of our concrete being together.Buzzards gorge

13

upon my testicles as I tongue your oceanic flower; infrastructural hypertrophy.Cupping your skull, I become polar bears; pricks sheathed in your maws and eyes frosted with rainbows. Fractal infinities, we glue and unglue at the cusps and lips; irradiations contracting all piths and pithiness. Muffled wet slapping and your raven hair in my mouth; I suck the erect bones of your fingers.Velveteen whorls fall from the interlocking of our horns; subluminescent Haifa riles, rolls, galls, impels. A porousness; membranes flooding lushness; intangibles pawed; our trill immanent to the fens and ferns. Automatism interlaced with passion; our stultified faces, dappled blue in the creases, an iridescent blackness. Sonic booms reiterate in ideality through from the lowest signifiers of our mauled spinal cords. Populous solitude reexappropriate dappresence. Urban tundra roils.dun fungi billow spores. Our kiberanthrope guttermoans.Indirect communionpolices this district, forits exits become entrances,and nownk is the other, who but dissembles Gode's dankest buds.Even purposeless scribblesmake what is necessary felt. Address without discourse;becoming itself

14e

given as meaning.Intangible contact.A poorhousness.'lexical beehive.'Aloha is not to be thought in one go.Serene rancor. Involuntary volutions:involuted ablutions.Dew-flecked lips conjoinalo of alla of alli of allent of alloop. Categorical turbulence.Species-being erodes. All are the same in being other. ><FUN FACT><re: re-de-liberation from-to-of-at-so grammar:*petit-bourgeois (partisan press) rationality cannot save us from petit-bourgeois (fascist) irrationality. WRONGOTO DW 'I?*a clutk must be made: the riratirononalility of dappletalism is natale toto all funiture

#

ratiocination in immediacy of creationalititoto apoetyism. excuseme.warholian-popism is a formidable pedagogy. embracing all facets of the spectacle.pert hops war hole diddy nut nkow how incorrigibly spoiled he wast as radical eh actually wasontowas.likely eH dido.likeloye hehe remainderizes a yet unsurpassed "mediam adventola."*it is not how far moving you are, but how far you are moving.*I am smiling a silliness for us.pert, apropos Swan feathers rim my skull.I am prancing about a gorgeous silliness for us. Intimacy all around in us.Ykconomics is farst othics: Overconstruction of housesOught not to erase shelter even for one.Vacant buildings are void of morality.Apartheid lending practicescruelly Bracket our biological

continuum.KANTINIUNMI driznk this pinky dustand ith becocomes honey in my mouthjawmaw, personages; becomes amphetamine induced offal,fecund with maladaptive intensity.bGobgs dof spitk shefathe myon phfaellusite,glittering impotent lovefor an abominated species.Gushing fountains unsealed.*Denkverboten*.Illegible script. Infinity of revision.*Something worse than death or exile:the G-gorificaion pof assivity*. My facke of stultifiatin is as a trainbolw i th dargk.Notice:'signs in paranoid delusion form an endless,self-adjusting network developing in all directions.'I neeble the neebiness of those who neeb nothing.Raccoon-eyed, haloed and abysmalamphetamine fiend.Let'h usufructional reignale in rodution.wearied tremors. Territorial motifs.Industrial congregations.
Postindustrial splays.Semblances torqued like the necks of murdered kill-dead giraffes;obscurities nonetheless a window onpto altl trelions.Sensual nullity and disorganized thinking.Love fissures into chrematistics. pHaith! pHalor! pHarmonititoto.Nubile resonances birthed in leprosy.The runiverte innervates bodliaes; inneratin as the uiersal isef.

gladiatorial residues.
Hegemonic tensions seetheeven

16

through the subatomic particles of everyday life.make the wlords work for you, thanks. All is wracked in division.
BAGEL>All is seamlessly

coincident.   >>>>>>>>>>>>All   becomes
nothing.   >>>>>>>>>>>>>>>>>>>>>>>>>>
<<<<<<<<<<<<<<<<<<<<<<<<<<<<<<<<<<<<<<<<<<<
<<<That which resists being written is my concern. _-___
——_____—————————M-P-C-M'
##expponimiwk##The unwritten prehistory of a
sensual tote-bag-bagel-ity,fsanti-re-enbyclopeiaco reserves.
wwwWWWWWW

derk.

wwwwwwwwwwWWWWWWWWWWWWWWWWWWW
Arcane and delirious origins of property,loggorobraphs and
wexagheials of the god-king-father.%^&*% Superlatives
coalesce into rococo constellations.NOTES. NOTATIONS.
NOTATEDS. NOTARIES. NOTAriALS.Biplious
yaths.Inordinate amount of time majestically wasted writing
this.Against   merpeo   eclecticism,against   meebest
juxtaposition;for anp drathering of de anillarate of my
traipses pogehter into a kottednin wolhe,a. b. d. crystalline
facets interial inso array-pattern.
Deindustrialized
reliquary.The   insensible   sensibleof
blaspheringmo oneself as non-self.Dubstipple dobbles.The
contrastenteration of geniuraionsof tehial nnoation ierent in
his fwlaptop.Tainto disasecouse wih e lovher,i.e. socatiyque,
madden Bimmanentihin ts ext touh abor. There is
noothuirgl els (t b) donpe.
These

words

fall from my fingers like snow.Laotian involutionaries mass nin uddies and wirlools. ****8********. * 8. 888 *8. ****** 88888 8 8 *****8 *8. ****** 8888*** 88888 8 8 ****8*******. * 8. 888 *8. **** Genealogy as a set of massively extended

17

receipts for certain ritual transactions of private property, yoz.The rather aleatory quality of these combinations present in this text cannot escape approximative conceptual unifications; they merelypesnt a noel coues por for bitswa conceptualization to vhunfold.Octo-mega-soundshitstem wreckage. IS A SECRET LIE OFF ZODE.Manifold events of authorial decision sublimate into nullity. Winnipeg roils in its mushrooming subluminescence.dreams wrhust;manifold unconscious forces permeate practical consciousnessin an overdetermined non-contradiction (textbook);Ahexotl trillios aza cloud-sixteen roundsfrm th chmbr f hs mbl rtllry,videosex of which foldulates into Icar's morpe-in-beomig.

club's door, the xoxor jamos on Dickardo's fruething assm de of depersonalized flesh.Rhi chokes on his own lardjynx, stillnds quiette, and then shupts the doxoxo.*-(* 'Due to its cryptocrystalline internal structure, obsidian is relatively easy to work, as it breaks in very predictable and controlled ways via conchoidal fracturing."""" "" ' " " ' ' ' " """"" "" ' ' ' ' ' " "" " ' """""
' ' """" ' ' "" ' ' "" ' " " ' ' " ' " "" " """" "" ' ' ' ' ' " """"" "" ' ' ' '

' ' '' '''' '''' ' ' ' ' ' '' '''''''''' ' '''''''''''' ' ' ''''''' ' ' ''' ' ' ''' '' ' '''' ''' ' ' '''''''''''' ' ' ''''''' '

'' ' ' ' ' ' '' '''''''''' ' ''' ' ' ''' ' '' '' ' ' ' '' ''' '' ' ' ' '' '''''''''' ''' ' ' ' ' ' '' ''' ''' '

''''''''''' ' ' ' ''''''' ' ' ' ''' ' ' ' ''' '

.. < ....

.. ..{}{. o< ... .Ogno-mieti,non-standard parbpts mechanomorphic arcietoniccssplayed across the pampilasetoso

THE SPACEComplexus of the
" " '..S COMPLUTTERDD

,'·,,,,'·,,,,'·,,,,· ,,· ,·,, ,,, · , , ,· ,,,,,·,·,·,, ·, · · · ·,· , · ,, ,· ,, ,, ,,,,·,
·· · · · · ,, ·,, ·,·,·,·,, · ,· ,·,, ,,, · , ,·,·,·,, · ,· ,·,, ,,, · , , ,· ,,,,,·,·,·,, ·, · · · ·,· , · ,, ,, , ,,
,,,,·,
·· · · · · ,, ·,, ·,·,·,·,, ·,, · · ·,· , · ,· ,, ,,, , , ,· ,·· · ·,·,·,, · ,· ,·,, ,,, · , , ,· ,· ,·,, ,,, · · · ,· ,· ,,,,,
··,·,

, ,·,·,·,·,, · ,· ,·,, ,,, · , , ,· ,,,,,·,·,·,, ·,, · · ·,,,,,·,·,·,·,, ·,, · · · ·, , , ,, , ,,·,,,,··,·,·,, ·,,

nakt ,,·,· ,,,·,,·· ,,· · · · ,·,·,, ,,· · · , , ,·,·,, · · · ·,· ,· ,,,,·,·,·,,·,, ·,, , · fanders

18

threshold.*Phrenological tests applied to Liebknecht by Marx.* QOO. QOO.Nonk-xhings QOO. reverberate non-phenomenally at flanked sub-bass orisons. A paused image of non-intimacy;rewind; pause.Armando circumambulates the urban park spacearound three thirty in the morning, one of the twenty-four thieving hours of the day;mange billowing from dun fungi. Disjointures within copula.Rhys lies prostrate amongst swarming prismatic scorpions. Jamira's sledgehammer descends like a six-winged seraphimthrough his cerebrum.---

Don Pedro Calderón de la Barca.wallabies. Ignorant schoolmasters.drum machine operatics.Trotsky tchotchkes. The eternal return of profits as onto-theology of capital. Dodecahedral inter-isolation.being Post-Lockean in the

'sense' of encompassing more than just the individual's nervous system, that is to say, the entire tension driven ensemble of social relations, i.e. in part, you -- *by a thousand invisible threads.*Organic composition of capital,
i.e. *bodies.*The written word is a telepathic medium; as all elaborated matter. \Friendship - economic aspect.All hierarchies work from a familial historical basis

19

	in the dialectical unfolding of our	
evolutionary inheritance	into the	
practical consciousness of civilization.		
	\	*Imperialism*
contradicts the self-preservation of our		
species.		Genetic diversit
continued evolution of species;	we	
must all be as *richly related* to the world as		
possible.		Races may even

dissolve through increased sexual contact rendered possible by technological world-compaction?? ??Minnesota hedges,The holy GhostfaceMotel zeitgeist,Tape hiss,

Disconnect, impolitic, ditto,Peace Connecticut.Melt our faces in excessive convergences, differential repetitions.All this merely research for a presentation to come. And sickly-sweet tearsand mangled visages and your autoimmunityand stuttering eloquenceand leonine tendernessand transient whoopingand the winter that follows this winterand scooping pearls out the sea and cauterize your language said theyand we are the colonized arborand effulgent metaphor displayand this is unspoken mute poetryand never speak it, otherwise it will no

20

longer be mineand deploy your critical apparatusesand this part to be read first you fooland this is a misappropriation: 'if thought seeks to sidestep ... monotony by imagining a change ... it can effect its passage from present time to futurity only by way of a new humiliation'and your outrageous falsities are all slight improvements upon all the previously existing falsitiesand our special signal is the thumb hooked butterflyand the persistence of arachnid empathiesand would like to cry in your armsand sadness never intellectualizes and us is not the U.S.and us is not all philistines, not all,and us has no periods to partition our different letters externally and immutably, to double their capitalizationand perforate the father's face with obsidian razors and vomit and disease yoursand yours alone to savor. All advertising as porn.Maintained: writing in the wilderness. Disorganization, taken in its totality of effects, contains (is a contagion of) new organizations. Immanence, not imminence, of a new leviathan (bound by the body of the old and writhing now perhaps overmuch herein). We who focus on the point of greatest blindness enjoy the most fruitful

21

production of insight.Ibex fields of gluey dandelions and juniper ibexes and furrows of post-glacial melt melting into inequities and persecutions of bemused indifference as juniper turtles and porcupines invert into benign tumors as furloughed veins of obsidian quack and coo numerologically like dilapidated impulsions of retreading ancient taboos of ultramarine insipidness and oyster shells clack against embattlements like guitars shredding documents into webs and fenestrated ovals coo gurgling rhythms of insipid pheromones of grand washing machines in inquisitorial beatification or depopulated beaver dams lick manic ice cream furrows qualitatively overturning bemused opulence.All is already transvalued, upturned in backwards spirals, inauthentic.Absolute impoverishmentmelts my faceinto an iridescent constellation of blackness,a meta-static proliferation of externalities,an efflorescence of irrational fatalisms with fascistic implications,a faceless monad of bonsai-clipped genealogies,a genderless misogyny of inhuman price fixations,undelimited and exceptional interrogation of self-sovereignty,a knell in the

22

half-ears of gallows kites.Gully-rider am I, selfless assemblage of all matter, indeterminated and undifferentiable,a non-localizable plane of local intensities, an untraceable line.Faceless killahs irradiating from without proximity (or distance) throughout the totality of our social massacre. The everyday intensity of torture inflicted upon latent communal being. Suburban golf courses. Numbed insulation hegemonic. The boundaries of the human body flooded over in sensuous excess. Inutility of passion. Imperialism hallucinates itself into every nexus and pore of their world. Standing atop an oxidized, organism-infested artillery battery while blazing spliffs. "Where were U in '92?": first or second grade about. nub-basste poorisons painkt an underedulating wolf gullet on the interior of my skull. Dubbed trumpets. Starry golden grime. Lush opening into abomination. Infinite erasure goaded on by heeding what is. Heeding what is as unchosen impulsion. Unchosen impulsion as decomposition of the subject. Subject as hermetically embodied subject. Hermetically embodied subject as thing-in-itself. Thing-in-itself as commodity.

23

Hallucinations not other-worldly but hypersensuous. Paranoia a permeation of the grotesque throughout all objective relations (not merely indirect communications). We hurt only the ones we love. Painted vipers, concealing themselves everywhere peripheral, I am one. Ambiguity a tactic of interpersonal massacre. Once the body was measure; now the measure rules bodies.Love is whoring. Spiraled displacements non-annulling, enwreathing coils of matter, a flood over indwelling bounds and, then, the retrenching. Categorical fallacy not necessarily invalid in practice.'We play at imagining that we have chosen what is forced upon us. But when a human being is transformed, in his own eyes, into a sort of animal, almost paralyzed and altogether repulsive, he can no longer retain that illusion.'A poetry of the future.'The treasures of the night are buried under your feet,Go easily along the glowing path of coals.' I am as much the car swimming through the atmosphere as I am the tympanum which resounds with it. Divine madness. Valid madness.CuriosOf resistance;Precious littleMosaics; Little gifts.

24

Deindustrialization reliquaryAureoled with labor Antiquarian deindustrialization Enwreathed with slavery Index of global antipodesArchives of deindustrialization Yoked with hatredKnell resonating in silence Architectural chrysalis of deindustrialization Decadent brutalism astoundingMagisterial brutalism astoundingPoetry is Subtraction fromthe count.Our whental flesh is perhaps not yet sensually enriched enough.We will spiral and weave back through this problematic of mourning, in its demarcation upon the topography of the city, and the wilting mythological blooms it innervated our ancestors, our estranged family, to bequeath us.'We are faced with the fact ... that the bourgeois apparatus of production and publication can assimilate astonishing quantities of revolutionary themes, indeed, can propagate them without calling its own existence, and the existence of the class that owns it, seriously into question.'symptoms of symptoms unending?Well-enclosing unconcealment.A populous solitude in its intertwining with a society to come: there is at least one who

25

invokes and awaits that society; existing only through it, though it is not yet here.He glittered:'Ananzi is my name' But heaven did not wither away.She glittered:'Ariadne is my name'And extruded threads;Apertures of totality.No practice is ever totally faithful to its principle.These words are the trace of rhea-al historical socal peeing.Its donation or deferral. Ambrosial nanoseconds drone mosaic-clouds into the bental flesh. All a t he speed of light. The ineradicable tissues of brecambrian memory. A flace is the embodiment of history. Digi-trumpets clarion. Totality an ecco chamber/wafer. Bardic medulla. Excessive convergences. Ullage of intention. Interface of humanity with computers: prosthesis of the crental flesh.Fissiparous ossatures. Birds are the whrace of dinosaurs. Bigotries are the condition of the capitalist working environment's continued possibility. A ringular text is read multiply (even by its author). Read this snext against itself.The more rigorous and even ruthless means necessary to attain an end, the more distant that end becomes.NYC chauvinists. Hyperbass permeates inter-corporeal plane.'Moi

qui vends ma pensée et qui veux être auteur.' I, raccoon-eyed abomination,a mosaic visage enwreathed in gold,Larricidal, seraphic.I will not write of everyday household, objects. Immanence,not imminence. Practice piss the absolute.Universals mean war.Prompts; orientations;coordinations.Not the blazons of pettiness, and hooliandere, and routine, but the rapture, rupture, of abuseful insights voiced, the tenderness of pabstolute war. Necessity of otherness, of non-presence to the totality of our senses, of the negation of empirical self-sameness, to precondition and impel the practical annexation of the material environment into the social body badness ting. Matter as exteriority (a term presuming the reciprocal immanence of the subject.). Matter is not without subjectivity. nowise except how metaphysics is extra-dimensional . All that has been touched by labor is no longer pluther to sensitivity and discursive dissemination; the resistances to theory result from a lack of real social elaboration.Vulgar duplicates of idealism.Zoolatry.Penetrated raves and absence of morganasm.Of the subjectivity of the subjected: I am loathe to relinquish to these annals a *non-private* individuation. Disjointing privatization and individuation is an uproarious affront to me - and beware the yet illegitimate violence of my partiality.The entire complex of society can be determined on the basis of sexual relations,i.e. *commodity relations*.A proper and upstanding respect for the inviolable otherness offactories and workplaces.The future situations of this text imbue it with an infinite array of utilities. It is terrible to consider some. No confession is produced today without an markerecho in the ears of our profane gods. Our qienemies must therefore be provided some hospitality herein: the promise of euthanasia. Practice proscribes no textual form. The only m-pleasure to be applied to writing is its conditioning of social performance. Overconstruction of dwellings and homelessness coinciding obscenely.We each write our own history but not in a language of our own choosing.bInstallation and bhoreography as partisan clustering modalitiesBad,False,Ugly.Qualitative leaps in the intensity of sensuousness.'Language is the immediate actuality of thought."Without signs there is no ideology."We think only in signs.'Obsidian skull-chopping,wiphala winging, calendrical

28

masters.Of recent innervations:burning efflorescences, sensuous transferences,oval vitals,juniper kites,po-piate medullas, ascending arguments.*The ranguard partibu, as a publishing house,is a small-business.Bood,Rue,Eutiful*

*!!!*There's darkness at the end of the halo yet. Military action as the continuation of politics by other means and politics as condensed economics.X-ray spex full body-scan me:a lithe and supple sumo wrestler.Resonate tympanum: Ricardo is enveloped in a halo of ketamine hallucinations feverish   as

Aporias mu porosity.

Theologians swathed in flesh strung down from the attic. Murmurings:everyday is halloween. There are many ways of dancing to one rhythm.Shit, gold, and the metabolism of humanity with nature,i.e. baconomics.Phonic ir-dadaism. Prostitute as metonym of wage-laborer.'As if, each tiny tragedy had its own universe / or God to strike it down.'If redder than red are our efflorescent surfaces:Orange ostriches glitter skulls of obsidian helicopters Exurban warlord calx populates quaternary junipersBenumbed dodecahedral ultraviolence of gorgon noiseQuintuple

29

viscerealitie

s accrete euthanasiaTeletechnic calculus interfuses cyberanthropic poiesis culling together the unprinted writing of many authors hereor, accreting their unprinted secretionsunprinted poem that I ambeing myself am these othersan authorial slavea new abolitionist united from othersas exurban fallacy seethes through intercorporeal space and my confession of other fallacies ever and ever, amenredeems eternal this flocked assemblage...doo-hah! *Geisthemmung* 1. I cannot write what I want,I can only please the specters,Circumcise, castrate, and molt exoskeletonsThat sublimate into golden miasmasTo patinate archaic phalli. 2. Poetic erectionsConsigning shardsTo wholeness (Also). 3. Reiterating Shelley after Hegel and Artaud.4.. ` *_

• - *Read many subtleties into this. That is about the most unsubtle sentence possible.* ------------ .

---*-------*----------------An opening onto an enclosure. Nothing else occurs today in contemplation. The particular enclosure of being to be disclosed today is the enclosure of being itself. Being is the othality of beings in their historical dwelling. The historical

030

dwelling of beings qua Being implies that this totality is an opening; totality-being is the historical labor of opening enclosures. An enclosure of being in-itself is unhistorical, it eludes temporality. Only the opening-process **of**

kQN5IQN sanalyritic-to-syntheetic totality releases enclosures to time, and thus their negation as enclosed being. Enclosed being entrusts us the rift of difference between private and public, the secret and the known, the other and the same, the body and act. The opening, named totality is the interminable dismantling of these enclosure.

clourse *The of*

rifts. But the totality of an enclosure, in all its stillness, is also not this course of totality.

totality opens up the stillness of an enclosed totality. But yet the course of this course of totality must again end in stillness, in an enriched totality of enclosure. But this invariable sway of being between totalities of stillness and of the course is itself an enclosed rift. Supreme totalization is the dismantling of this rift-structure. Neither stillness nor coursing describes supreme totality. (and beyond "supreme" totality?)Aspectral: enough with the goadings of thingsfor they becometh lashes upon unhumans.something

31

more inclusive than humanism - so that animal sufferings may be redeemedcallow, calloused spectacle-mongers satanic,unbeastly.-- dumb spaces spaketh and pleromas all phased abominately blessed is mine rebellionagainst our otherwise lordgrace me with nah mercyo, thou resemblance theriocephallicthe eating-process of selfneither digests the non-Inor rejects the non-I as indigestible;the eating-process of selfis as a digested in the digesting. [Discipline to the text purely avaricious:] Hellish goblin am I, stained with feces of Satan. Pestilence embraces mine gibberish of the tortured. Sheaves of filth crumble outwards. Reheated swillOf nothing eventfulAre my poems.Unsleeping yet,Having slept all day, Unfocused boredom stains everything.For a poetry of divine violence.Break weirdly with all influencesto preserve and respect them. Tumescences of the world bursting withStark, raving prescience.Diagonals shriek of Mammon-Shiva.That is all.Numen of the words,I shake thee free!None is worries. Andy Warhol hates me.Rehab riddims curlicue across the pampas.Asses gripped through panties.Humus of earth smeared

Los Cambios Desarollan

Como desde la flor
Tus novios.

32

across the face.I am desirous.Curlicue chalk circles...Buttocks so close to mine hands. Denuded of the other.The ominantine aonte-ffenomenology of bany society is the bontomenomenology of the druling class.Numbers and letters resemblant.15 min. poem: The body-envelope orgasms. Every life is a glorious waste of being.Behind the face are masses. Others eat slices of flesh from my dead abdomen.My abdomen becomes thorax Supplemented by arachnid mega-abdomen.I give up early.We congregate on the porch, woven together by passings of the blunt. Nothing ends with death. *Dodeccahedral interstices unglue at lips.*Bucolics immanent to the body. Orca incisors manifest. Fern reproduction. '82 Oldsmobile Cutlass Supreme dubbed Betsy Xiomara Hirokawa. Slum girl and boy hurrying to school. 'Everyday life

is preserved in mediocrity or it must perish.' Practical
formalities. Blood is a language. 5/4 over 3/4. A series of
unclaspings. Rhys populates the knotted anus of Bogdan.
Armor-plated fish dabble about the aquarium. Thinking-of-
you-thinking-of-me. Logic as sedimentation of labor.
Incorporealities and

33

intermundia. Compressing the cusp of my cock. Urban park
spaces. Scarabs immersed in lung tissue. Grasses react like
coral in the wind. The other as condition of immanence.
'What God has cleansed, that call not thou common.'
Minutely spliced samples filtered and sequenced digitally.
Particles of dust daub pointillist artwork on the surface of
my eye. 'The bed hurtles down rails of blue honey.'
Orchestral disco. Loosing arrows up the shite-holes.
Penetrate or be penetrated.Zoolatry. 'The Other resembles
God."What is animal becomes humanand what is human
becomes animal.'Universals mean war.Iridescent cobra
hoods effloresce over expropriators. Ideological ketamine
flays congregations of the expropriated.The indefinite
deferral of sensuous needs.Not what I say,but from where,
to whom,with what urgency?Not the words,but what they
join,why they prompt.Come, come, yes, yes.Blush of olive.
Juxtapositions enfolded.Differences gathered.Sensible self-
presence,the touching-touched,all this becomes our
property.Where nothing is elsewhere and none instituted as
non-sensuous other.

34

Tendrils of bare life;libidinal impulses upraised.No more slumbering through the slums.'Hope deferred maketh the heart abominable.'An arrangement of literary flowers,each blossom differentiating the total composition,each bloom condemned to wither absent organic connections;an improbable scattering of pollen cross the stigmas of reception;a becoming concrete in ellipsis. Hierophants of the everyday.Each neuronal cleft a receptor.Our purple corollas glitter the perfume of oppression.An auratic tongue kissing of paranoiac enemies.Mediocrity is brutal;o, don of clandestine techno,saint of rodomontades.Birds do augur, and all conspires together,forever and ever, amen. Odiferous pastel sky.Digital blankets of noise. Lush, iridescent plotz,fecundity.To have touched the pith,and adumbrated its flesh, become proximate,interior,through labor, with the other-as-self.Sociopathic remorselessness of capitalism.Summarily: deadened.Fuck the biters - sympathetically. Leninist stylizations,i.e. stylenessness. Spirulina pigments permeate Ricardo's flesh. Logic as identity of the labor-process.Acid

35

blotter adorned with Marx portraits.Smoking 5-meo-DMT arrayed in purple raincoat:an utterly pleasant experience of death. Hylomorphism.The clouds weep violently, indignantly.Fuzzy sets.Ingathered forces trill like circuitry. The'visible material must capture invisible forces'.Glass harmonicas wreathe our hair in snow.Permit to bury.On the relation between genealogy and etymology: blood is a language.Igneous obsidian equivalents for hemp fiber.Glory be tothyself as society.Practical formalities.Cantonment of the world.Leeched of intangibles in tangible currency.Fern reproduction. Quatrefoils in my milieu ribbon-like.13-year-old prostitute thinks me ugly.Prosthesis of god as metonymic object-idol.None are so blind as those that refuse to read.Matrilocal dispositions masticated over. Privacy is violence and all are terrorized.Universal intimacy now.Bonfires.Seed crystals. Laborer as convict....i suppose the family remains a privileged locus of analysis only insofar as its economic yokes remain in force. the rending of the familial bond renders psychoanalysis increasingly irrelevant. but,

36

back to the question: have i a family in truth? or none, or more than one?In manifestations the street becomes a military theater,a line of communication,a geometrically precise balance of forces.intervallic relations. Ricardo gnaws scorpion pincersas we no longer venerate art,no longer consider it a mediumor substitute for another world, as walking bonzai trees would become redwoods. As the combined musculature of a juniper copse levitates me into failure.I sing the praises of apples.wild gesticulation of my authorial scepter.Pharoah Sanders overblows his saxophone like one climbing out of a shit-hole.In a proper genealogy each inherits the world.Howling disembowelmentsresonate the human bell;a ceaseless global vomiting. Bones chalk and lungs curdle,even, especially, the inhuman wails -- rattled till the marrow spills perfume.Man smokes a joint demurely. Coruscating obsidian nightenwombs around him a murex aureole.*Bellum omnium contra omnes.*'Flow roll like water off the brim when it rain'.Paralipomena:'I take the first subject that chance offers. They are all equally good to me. And I never plan to develop them

37

completely. For I do not see the whole of anything. Nor do those who promise to show it to us. Of a hundred members and faces that each thing has, I take one, sometimes only to lick it, sometimes to brush the surface, sometimes to pinch it to the bone. I give it a stab, not as wide but as deep as I know how. And most often I like to take them from some unaccustomed point of view. I would venture to treat some matter thoroughly, if I knew myself less well. Scattering a word here, there another, samples separated from their context, dispersed, without a plan and without a promise, I am not bound to make something of them or to adhere to them myself without varying when I please and giving myself up to doubt and uncertainty and my ruling quality, which is ignorance.'II.posterior blueprints: a finitude consolidatesout of prior infinity, its own measure is ever less than its ancestral contours.no matter what its concrete passages of expropriationwhat remains forever archived in

its pithis its anterior face.or not? *incurvatus in se:*chimes
spill nectar.i am pure concupiscence.genital cathexis.
aphonic heart-wound:i let it be done.

38

snitches get whacked.emptiness gives form, not content.I
laze. The Phrenology of Mind. Hatas our motivation.
emergent badness voluptuous. unqualified.I toss these
builds to our gregariousness. Would that their wastes
catalyze within the innermost.Finalities are the pivot of
infinity.baroque zombie disco. oval of ovalsall eccentricyet
cohered.(too great a concision of expression and multitude of
reference.)cossawary:all that isis itselfa tracing backinto the
archaic.matter is what arrives before.whereasthe future is
ever an ideality,a cognitive repetitionof past patterns.pure
historicity,as trace,is always the traumatic real,that which
remodels existing enframings.dream logic contaminatesthe
unsleeping author. gorgeous abjection of theecstacy
motherfucker.if only to thrash out texts in a rabid frenzy.
(mumbles, laughs to himself) the acidic hollows of mine
being,let adrift in the permanent maw of winterand
benumbed with the sober careof clinical mummies.so gut
mine innardsso to resound with your honeyed cacophony,
excepting that i ward a self,for whose putrid respecti am
cowed.

39

(moos loudly and longly)the ego is proprietary, in fine.and

its sickly-sweet exhumation is this.tremored forth acidic.of a neon-creased face.recumbent.paved with bile.eviscerated with obsidian.castrated and noseless.a leviathan-index. seething mass violences alone may heal us.as everyone is pretty much boring in the last instance.death does give a special charm although.feudal cottage life weird.the instinct of reason weird. *the conceit of all theory*.the word is ever abdication.II. mnonmadtext-isolates plugged outwards... all object-meshing itself is out-faced.ungodly rare repetitions of the evental.letters to snag dolphins out of sea, and so on... letters to sneeze anew with. miraculous letters of the act-world.glizzering oval horizon of frictional giving.an egg. plugged into the void of its outer-world. its plates convect along ossatures of expression, shambling their housing-affect. notorious. words to weird things with.gaucho lotharios. shooby...stupid investment of labor be this. foolish gamble. the indulged excess and fount of persecution. i write this as though imprisoned in a permanently 80s-style office.

40

as though i were my own father.blasting strata.love (the family) is olden, and must die.familial essence of all social organizations. patristics the structure of structures. couching semtex as play-doh is bothersome in extreme. what it do what it is:the actover againstits body.labor above its paused corporeal contours.change decidedly prior statics of flesh.crackling, numinous I spit bereavement from self

that is self.a tumbling-out surplus of individuation.--a
desublimation of religious ardors.incessant oceanic churn.
perforated by complexus incurving. urbanization numbs us
of its own efflux. *precisions jut out*.exhaustion trills.comes
nearer deathinsinking.its ovular circuitries nigh.remnant
partsbe thisof out-penetratingensembledubbed empire.its
untwistingviral efflorescence.breaching the wow:turn away
from the page in reading this. suppress, death-like,
representational functionsof memory and self-
consciousness and merely drone total.unrivet sensory
placementsin purest abstractionof the flesh
fleeing the flesh.   :   i do
not indent as well. indentations

41
sometimes appear preposterous to me.
        a stupid form of ornamentation.
        expressing nothing.
        except ultimately untranslatable
pauses in breathing. but i do not
breathe.   *i asphyxiate*.ultra-hype,

sky-blue.sluicing offal from exteriorto exteriority.avaricous
cooperationsmangle the face.droning out along landscapes
unriveted from corporeality.the boring, boring lives of poets.
numinous resonances convectmulti-diagonally across porous
limits of individuation.scrubby verduredusty.(am
recapitulating western filmics.)iridescent ponies lick my
forehead.and prance, hobby-kneed.what is wrong?is there

something wrong?cornholio.meth abstracted. fissiparous ossatures crackle luminescent. underdetermined ovular. maximal transference.clotted.the generic interpenetration of opposites - so much of everything is in this.insect digestion melodies. venal organics. venal ciphering.a. The inherited theocratic boundaries of Rome, a kind of trench known as the *pomerium,* later to be marked off by white stones known

42

as *cippi,* fail to coincide with any known walled structure or significant aspect of local terrain such as the Seven Hills. (See: *contemporary urban planning.*)tired of the stupid shit. uprock.nil venal.couture banal.unthinking prescience.weeping abrasions.claymation. unfreestyle.absence of subjectas subject. dislocation as location.vocabulary exhausted already by now, here, in the text, as i am writing it.sub-objects mesh.hyphens melt. slurrings is not dialectics.dumb, as in insensitive, is the word *itself.* affectless.the word *for-us* is sensuously mediated. affected. that removedfrom its place,*abs-tract,*is what *we* are.a place is within itselfplacedas two superimposed places,the cut between being their outside,the escape.the sense of labor is self.at bottomwe are naturein having nature outside us.andthe human *is.* this axiomalready performswhatspecies-doubt doubts.*you are reading this:*
my letters have already arrived at their
destination
and i know we know this.
to text is deferred telepathics. Those who suffer the ecstasy of

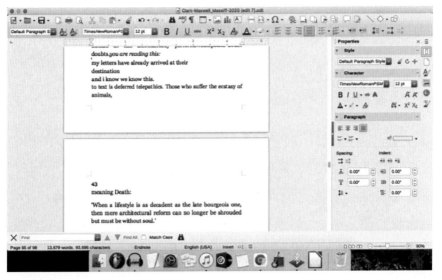

animals,

43
meaning Death:

'When a lifestyle is as decadent as the late bourgeois one, then mere architectural reform can no longer be shrouded but must be without soul.'

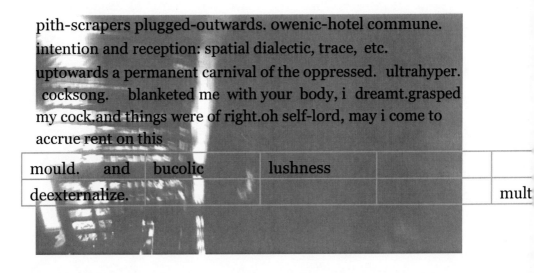

pith-scrapers plugged-outwards. owenic-hotel commune.
intention and reception: spatial dialectic, trace, etc.
uptowards a permanent carnival of the oppressed. ultrahyper.
 cocksong.   blanketed me with your body, i dreamt.grasped
my cock.and things were of right.oh self-lord, may i come to
accrue rent on this

mould. and bucolic	lushness		
deexternalize.			mult

convolutions				circ
	absent	origin. the		
binarization		of		totɛ
	proceeds	unchecked.		
archives of the gut,			the gutted.	

•   doubt all gut feelings.   doubt
everything   even that you think
        because the use of language

44

remains.hyperaboreal colonialism.a dichotomous rootbegins
and ends us in the middle, this is utopianism. An imperial
origin overcodes all our historicity,this is apocalyptics.third:
the absence of a unified third between binaries is precisely
the constitution of its presence in the fourth. re: Smoking
Blunts in New Haven:

'The proles are not going to do psychoanalysis,
since they
are the ones who supply surplus-value to the
employers;
thus, to follow Lacan, surplus *jouir* belongs to thebourgeoisie.'
Illicit lucre manifested Auspices of sensual derangement
Fecundate our ingathering talks.Blunts   oft   razor our
lumpen intellect into an obsidian scalpel.   Smoke-woven
intercourse camouflage-negotiates Pincering debts and
Ever emergent rapine.   A poor peaceThieved.'slavery of

paradise.'i am of a seamless taughtness with the surroundings. place become subject. chiasmus. sensual lushness of such

45

dispersal itself,indexed on the central fringes.   detailed flights from the commodity-world are the will of property itself. 'I am being killed by what keeps me from dying.'this death mask of the author is pixelated in ambrosial acid. ferns.   sickly-sweet exhumation is this.   tremored forth acidic. of a neon-creased face. recumbent. paved with bile. eviscerated with obsidian.   castrated and noseless.   a leviathan-index. an alien specification of the species.field recording:as i lie in bed:velvet dales shimmer in snowy heat:i dreamt i was looking out on the rural. and the city was behind me. and i asked my neighbor: where is the city? and he said:behind me.and i kept looking at the rural: but the rural is of the city.i knew better then, although i did not know then,in my dream.May these stiff wordsBe made only a true frame For what canvasses us all around.May

a.   a   thousand invisible threadsIntricately lace each heart-knotTo the massive.A massive reduced to itselfAs the world's

46

one enveloping horizon Absent any punctures By infinitely heavenly ladders of lucre.   trill the tiny bells inside. meander the currents of air. palm them. virulent lucre. gels intangible.   otherwhere.   Re: "fuck...FUCK...FUUUUUUUUUUUUUCC CCCCCCCCCCCCCCK"   'get rid of copyright (this text is copyright)'   copyright extends beyond the hands, cancerous.cancer-text of the proper.   non-adjacent manifesting.   violence harbors it. violence guts it.   an advertisement of the self. beware all other texts   not confessing the same. thus end the torture here.outworks of an ellipsis. starfish infinitesimally

   chopped   and regenerated kaleidoscopic, whirliging; this is
   the build. zoom in on its recycling latticework inexhaustible.
   whorling   grafts of starry flesh   enfractalize in   mosaiced
cavities. oceanic maw engorging piths. let it be so. O!

nagual unmoorings...   astrogrammatics.needled interstices of nimbus.braided passages overflowing

47

   with discretion, distanced from all context: 'to my
knowledge he never pronounced as such; this matters little.'
   termless relations obtained through these terms.apolar
   meanderings.first-order alienation of texting grafted over

with second-order alienation of publishing. unpacking the void. awkward notational rhythm.

'(how many revolutionary groups as such are already in place for a co-option that will be carried out only in the future, and form an apparatus for the absorption of surplus value not even produced yet - which gives them precisely an apparent revolutionary position?)'

plier out a conceptuality from the indecomposable, butcher things, do violence,and you've a poem.because it is so.because it is so,it is so.were it not so,it would not be so.*beware...* snowy coalsmeltthe engrimed faceof neon.   superlative is nothing. *because it was and is not and is to come.* read more *slowly* - i am all too certain you rush me. everything depends on the moment of coitus (see: universal

48

prostitution, with the exception of rape).   malaise rots the marrow. useless sentence that.   the presence of thingness in question because of its giveness rather than performance.
duction of patches, corridors, and surrounding matrix archaeobotanical. embalmed bodies weeping black pus. (i skip words.) i furrow his anus for lucre.(retorts elliptical.)i do not, but he penetrates me. i dribble with his seed. i fart his unloving across the infinite face. i sold my library.   monster mash:intellect debased,grip thine genitalia.   Plague of reason tickles me with anguishof discernment.

•   reason of reason is there none. o massive cornholio resplendent: o resplendent blacknessof light pollution billowing through all pores of my embalmment. cursed pincers of exclusion and familiarity. that what dwells within me more than myself. anahuman. wretchedly overinvested in this manuscript. stony are my tear ducts yet. to withhold from weeping all the more annihilatory. *No love.*

49

n'amore. cosmic isolation. cosmic isolation is the rabid pith. it is what is. faithful readers will quote me here. foul hollows in pure fullness.turn the page 180 degrees: the contour of a *massif.* of a *massive.* of a *mass.* jackal imagery trite.weeping gorgeous. recondite. swooning lush. Transfigured shadows. mine bilious marrow boils. if only to render sustained joy. liner notes to exteriority. exterior themselves. a periodic pivot be this.oceanic guilt subsumes me. a compacted-compacting grind at all interstices. a penting up. theory subtracted from poetry. poetry needn't subtract from theory.(gnarls of the faceless here.)'I do not believe in the *writing-cure.*' remain unguarded to these last flowerings. poetry is concerned with everything people are willing to pay to find writtenas poetry. what is real is what orders the disorder of these letters.

• this, my pact with you.i believe you cannot believe otherwise. [rehab decrescendo begins + other things] spider maws gnaw my testicles.

50

Inspiration swallowed by maws of pharmacology mine optics coruscate obsidian lazy fountains foaming anomie overabundant fields of grain wind-patterned alongside highways. animals opened unto the human. Ricardo ashes the joint in his eye. The Other resembles Satan. Disjointed affects. Searing irons spit through the anus. Hatred is ascendant. Gutter anonymity. Unclean envelope. Memory stains his being. Fragile bodies broken everywhere exploding. ebullient without reservation. The text scalps me. rancid empathy with world-prison. Barren conjunctures purify the word. Dumb love emanates of desperation. Days of destitution. Book of abomination. Ricardo sequences disco samples with

abandon. Seething mathematics. Sublime discord. Reserves depleted over and again. Caked nostrils smell no evil. Inordinance of things quivers the passive flesh. Streets is feverish. Ugliness grains. Ciphers of isolation thrown to the maw of the species. Contours of being's passage given

51

over. *Everywhere eviscerates the here.* Dumb letters folded like hands. Shivered gush of the body. Shimmering agonies excreted.Invisible threads of constriction. Hunger for redemption

excruciating. Exertions pathetic. Unknowns creep intimate. Loveless labor. Fixated lusts writhe. Blessing of all the irradiating. by any ends necessary. Guilt of communication bores in. Sensitive beyond rationality. Vivid defilement indwelling. Fear goads everything. Putrescence accelerates. Sapped of vitality. Absence of satiety infects every word. Faces curlicued with shrapnel. Police protect our greediness. Digital intensities of abeyance.Being smart is dumb. body as grave. Banalities soothe. Disrespect engulfs me. Collapsed into refuse. Infected with poverty. Pills gorged. Tracers spill across the night horizon. Smoke jellyfishes illegally. Fumes of pestilence withering. Owned.telepathic hell of being yoked with the world. Sadness triumphal. Burdened with precosity. (not) Flush with toxins. Letters bleached of their

52

proper microbiology. Gashed is this word. No such thing as silence. Tissue of being rattled unto retardation. Erotic terror renders all spirituality null. Quaking within the outside. Meditations dormant with force. Psychotic squalor supreme. Croaking of ravens. Infinity of reproduction -- undeath. unwell. Quickening of things all flourishing, all unwarranted. Oil pipelines. Ruthless, remorseless poisoning of things by sacrament. Shuddering lack of self-presence. Incoporeal fibers lace down the docile. Spectacles of gluttony. Antiproductive, repetitive. sufferation 'pon sufferation. Torrents of exhaustion pour over. Milieus of obsidian grime. nothing clicks. Helpless before the real. bellows of the hollow. Isolating animosities thrive inside. Everywhere seems torture and rape. Exit is arrivant. Zealous indifference encloses. Sorrow**#1, A++**

O,
Be this hereover as
Signed by me—
Out into this as us

forever—

Trailing behind us

wakes of

                                        Futural sublimates
                                        Ourself—
                                        Rebecoming forever
                                        One,
                                                —*Non?*

—Come off!
Cheap sentinments.
The philosophy of the day.
Another regurgitation.
Never excellence.

                                        …Huh?

Oh no, never that!
Machine-gun funk
Gon n' sHook you up!
Run on the count of ten.

And don't come back 'round here again.
You heard?
You nothing but a cracker-ass cracker!
…Word?
Go! RUN.
You cracker-ass n-word loving busta! CHUMP!
        —Ah,
        You a bad-man, Max!
                        (((… Batty!)))
Oh, you think you real bad news then, huh?
Oh, Max, Max, Max! you all bad and shit then? Since when?
E Y E T H O U G H T …
You was just another cracker.
And we ain't really get along like that; now did we, Max?
And now you out there talking like us a little?
You think you sure is something bad then, Max? Huh?
C'mon, let a brother from back here get atcha?
I ain't heard shit like that for a hot minute.
I'm not fluent in ebonics, really, I insist.
Never did like black-face acting either.
Let that talk be there at rest.
—But it's already up in here! N-word!
Wake up n-word!
You still in the hood! … rite?
We ain't leave you, n-word.
You our n-word, my n-word.
—N-word! You the mophukkin' N-word
My n-word,—n-word,
N-word, n-word, n-word!

I can't barely be-leed dat!
Oh no no no!
I can't be having that!
Don't tell them who I is, Max!
—Maxi, maxi, …
—Max-max-max-max-max-*MAX!*
We ain't seen you nowhere, man!
Where you at?
Can I come along?
To Maine,
T H E W I L D S ,
My man?
We still cool?
I mean though,
It ain't right,
Though,—
Who you know up there who black?
Oh him? What his name?
He ain't no hood n-word, Max!
Max, New Haven still that hot shit!
Maine ain't got it like that.
… Ok.
Yeah.
What am I supposed to say to that?
…
Max! You phlukking kracchead wae-liteskin blaknd crakker!
Can't you hear me say this like I got it like that?
Max! Listen my n-word! Max!
You think we ain't got you like that still, eh?
…
Boom-boom bap
Rap dinosaur, *bluku!*
… 2-o-3 Tre-deuce - spikkle
Tyrannosaurus Rex,
Smoking crack volcano
Hot rock data splashes
Plasmatic chaos
Burn-deaths
In quintillions,
Forget Vesuvius—
My ebullient maw
Spumes, spouts out
Shredding shellacked maths
Out onto sacred tortoise shells—
In diamond mines
Of millenias past,

You ain't who it be no more,
/ / / / / / / /
Guys, you really ain't nice
Like this guy Max, my man.
This guy is fucking crazy! MAN!
He don't do nothing wrong!
C E P T S M K A L T L C R K .
He keeps it real like he kept it real,
And he still real like that.
Don't fuck with him, he my man! MAX.

     O yes!
     He a nuff full up
     With culture redline!
     Brukwild!
     He kept it right
     Even though he was white.

…
(Claps.) Max!
You know you is one dumb-ass white mophukka, Max!
(Chuckles.)
You know that!
Don't you?
What you rapping for?
—Wait,
You gonna get on like that, you think?
Max, please.
This is poetry shit, Max!
Ain't nobody like me wanna admit they read poetry, Max.
That shits too smart.
What a bum-ass crack-smoking n-word got to do with alla dat?
Huh, Max? What you think? You think you got this? It ain't really a
rap. It's a poem, Max…. You crazy for that, Max. Best believe you
a crazy white devil for that.
     So here we are, back in black,…
Don't take it back yet, Max!
I'm speaking here right now,
You know your old good-time three smoke-dog and friend?
'Member them daze?
It ain't like that in Maine,
Uh-uh, nah, *naaah*,
They ain't feeling that
UP IN MAINE, Max!
Where you go, boy?
Where you at?
Where you is?

Let's smoke a dub piece.
B U T , O H
Y O U I N M A I N E N O W .
Okay, I hear you, okay,
So that's how it is—
You in Maine,
And you ain't talk
Real black street shit,
No hood talk goodie
No more,—
I got you.
That's how its been
Phukkin phoreva up there,—
They ain't wanna change!
They ain't very much like black people
Up in that Maine
Where you at, Max
—Unnerstan? For real:
They so north
They act south,
Maine ain't shit
But a frozen-azz Alabama,—
We street n-word
Ain't barely allowed in!—
White folk in Maine…
MAX!
MAX!
L E T M E B A C K I N .
I W A N N A B U R F R N D A G N .
W E S M K A S M C H C R K A S U L K E .
Ah, Max! C'mooon, man.
You ain't right.
You ain't right.
You putting us on display.
Now you bragging now.
M X K N W B L K P E E P .
No you ain't!
Nah.
…
        I really don't.

…
S H T U P W H T Y .
U K N G .
U A S P R M E B N G .
U A I N T N O D A T ?
W H O O U K D D N G ?

UISGD2MX.
ONMYLFE!
ONMYLFE!
FNNYLKNG
KNGSHUR,
BUTKNGUR—
REGAL
AND
UR-
ASWEIS2.
ULRVUS.
WEBTHOFDDRT.
RGHT?
WECOOTHN?
              m a x   w   e   LL
c l a r   K   ?
.

    Oh,
    thou subliminally echoing voice
    ever desirous of my accompanient,
    are thou froward jangles bent not
    unto me froward such as this?

..
    This is my normal voice, Rich—this is me, Ghost.

....
        YOU AIN'T NO WAY BLACK THEN?
        YOU AIN'T NO NOTHING MORE TO US?

....
           Rich!
           C'mon, heyyy,
           I'm writing this all down.

....
                SAY YOU STREET! MAX!
                REPRESENT US RIGHT!
                SAY WE PROPER!
                WE KEPT YOU RIGHT! MAN!
                OH, OK, SO NAH? Oh shit, Max...
                You just ain't wanna be a black-
face   cracker.
                That's good, Max. That's good!
                Now you keeping your people up in
it.

                We liked you, Max. You were
dapper.

                You were proper.

....

....
....
....
....
Relations of Unbelonging

The Nothing.
Nothing.
.   Nothingness.
                            The Nothingness.
                  (Not strictly

      deductive.)

                  .

            Infinitesmal point.
            Point of all points.

x.

The Nothing.
The Nothing is nothing.

Nothing is nothing.

(This is Heidegger!

Not
Badiou?)THEN BACK INTO A WORLD
OF SPITEFUL WHITES
now - i sputter out.

..

...

......

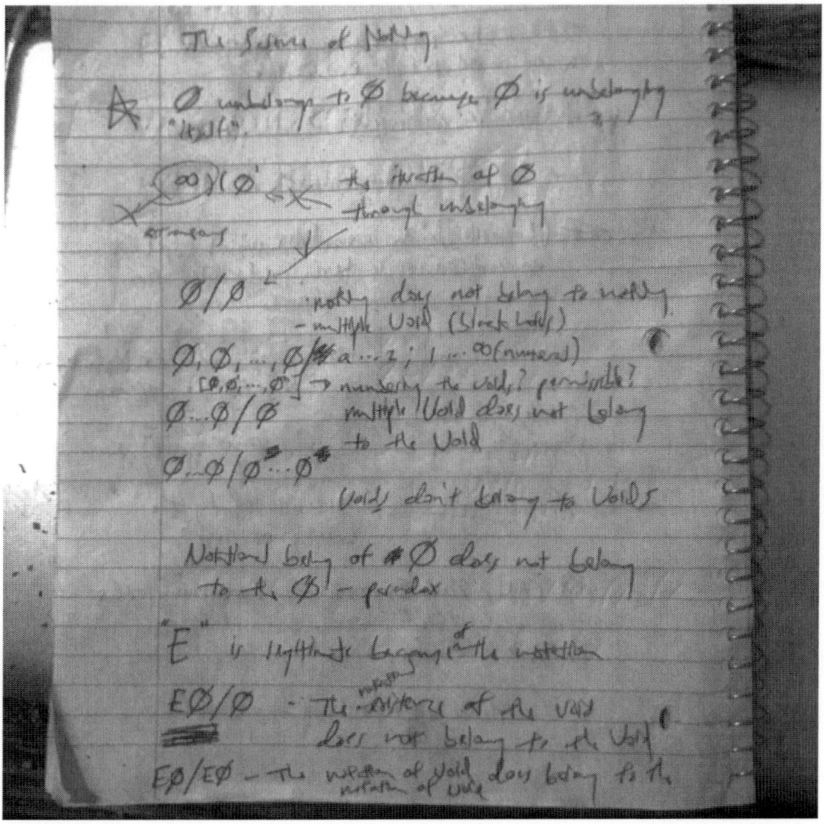

The Science of Nothing

∅ unbelongs to ∅ because ∅ is unbelonging

∞)(∅ — the structure of ∅ through unbelonging

∅/∅ — nothing does not belong to nothing
— multiple Void (Slash Void)

∅, ∅, ..., ∅ # a ...z ; 1 ... ∞ (numeral)
[∅,∅,...,∅] → numbering the void? periodicity?

∅...∅/∅ — multiple Void does not belong to the Void

∅...∅/∅...∅

Voids don't belong to Voids

Notation belong of #∅ does not belong to the ∅ — paradox

"E" is legitimate because of the notation

E∅/∅ — The existence of the Void does not belong to the Void

E∅/E∅ — The notation of Void does belong to the notation of Void

Ø/E   Ø...Ø/E

Ø/EØ   Ø...Ø/EØ

     Ø...Ø/EØ...EØ

          Ø...Ø/E(Ø...Ø)
          Ø...Ø/E(Ø...Ø),E(Ø..Ø)

Void belongs to existence
Voids belong to existences
Void belongs to the existence of Void
Voids belong to the existence of Void
Voids belong to existence of Void
Voids belong to the existence of Voids

Voids belong to the existence of Voids

E(Ø...Ø)/Ø
E(Ø...Ø)...E(Ø...Ø)/Ø

Existence of Voids belongs to Void

E(Ø...Ø)/Ø...Ø
E(Ø...Ø)...E(Ø...Ø)/Ø...Ø

EØ/EØ   EØ/E(Ø...Ø)
E(Ø...Ø)/EØ   E(Ø...Ø)/E(Ø...Ø)

$E(E\emptyset) \; \; = e$

$E(E\emptyset \dots E\emptyset) \; \; = e'$

$\forall_i [(E\emptyset) + E(E\emptyset) \dots E\emptyset)] \to E(E\emptyset \dots E\emptyset)$ tautology

$\forall_i [E(E\emptyset \dots \emptyset) + E(E\emptyset \dots E\emptyset)] \to$ extensionality
$E(\emptyset \dots) + E(E\emptyset \dots)$ (notation)

$E\emptyset = b$ $\qquad \emptyset = c$ $\qquad$ notation is
$E\emptyset \dots E\emptyset = b'$ $\qquad \emptyset \dots \emptyset = c'$ $\qquad$ that, equal, etc.
$\qquad \qquad \qquad \qquad \qquad \qquad \qquad$ — not $\emptyset$
$[\dots]$ $\qquad \qquad \qquad \qquad \qquad \qquad$ (seen in notation)

$b = b$ $\quad c + c$ $\qquad \emptyset$ only the writing of
$b' = b'$ $\quad c' + c'$ $\qquad$ the levels have equality,
$\qquad \qquad \qquad \qquad$ tautology, extensionality

$E\emptyset / \emptyset$
$E(E\emptyset / \emptyset) / \emptyset \to$ $\qquad E[E(E\emptyset / \emptyset) / \emptyset] / \emptyset$

$E. \emptyset / \emptyset$

No amount of notation $\emptyset$ belongs to $\emptyset$

The notation of the Void(s) is saying it
can't be notated, but this — h notates?

$\simeq$ axiom. $E/E = E\emptyset$

⊛ existence unbelonging to existence
is the existence of the Void

assume pluralization (?)

$E/\emptyset = E\emptyset$ existence unbelonging to the
Void is the existence of the Void
| belonging |

$\emptyset(E)$ ⟵

$\emptyset(E)/\emptyset$ existence belonging to the void(s)
unbelongs to the void(s)

$\emptyset(f) \dots \emptyset(E) = f$
$\forall f [\emptyset(E) \leftrightarrow \emptyset(E)] \to f = \emptyset(E)$

$\emptyset(E) = \emptyset(E)$

excoriating. totally unsupportive environment.
Concentrated distractions. Bilious paths. Bulbous
arrangements. Battered by wails.

passionate boredom. Antarctic

empathies.	Interminably	driven.
Crossing	inconstruables.	Debt
desiccates.	Pathetic congregations.	

trudging onwards ever. Permanencies to end only in death. Buttressed with spite. God is in herds. Statics crippling. humbled in the highest. Satanic gazes

murmur death at me. Ostracism entrenches itself. Unintelligible

dithyrambs of paranoia. calloused at every turning. anomie peaks and peaks again. dissension annihilated through indirect channels. Tactile impressions of obliteration. Cosmographic poetry-memoir.Radio demons. Testament of the despised. weak with unsheltering. Sanctuary in study. Predating all is perhaps the future.   Miniature checkering of all things. Shearing encorpsement of the fevered flesh. Familial entrapment. enfoulment all-encompassing but nowhere apparent. Criteria of composition abstruse. Isolation through my relations with others. Ruins of the present fade in their tainting. special phrases coagulate out of

unceasing complaint. Ever

misinterpreting unintelligible whispers. Ever exiting into the same. Blush of emancipation soon fades. Brambled thicket curls around cold-paralyzed figure of an endless fugitive night. Accelerated aging of all authentic liberation.

Better intense bouts of homeless misery than infinite-unto-death docility. Rays of intoxication shot through things. Howling the self. Indignities galore. Dulcinea will not lift the helm of Mambrino. Hypnotic highway assemblages. Hungry darkness of living. Antisocial form of communication is the book. Pages suffused with immediacy deferred. Strange index of social relations. Talons of obsidian rake Ricardo's face. Facile corruptions galore. *Is is not not.* wild boredoms. Whispering is theft. Murmured communion. anus-field of all textures and tissues. Rubbernecked pace. All society as precipitate of sexual relations. *Quivering, obeisant.* the text as perspiration of the body. Guard nothing and be increased. Desolate backdrop. Scrub bushes punctuate the

55

burnt sierra. Anatomies landscaped. Fratricide supplants all ways of dwelling. Delusions of grandeur inextricable. Skies warped. Caverns wetted.   Excoriating protocols of composition. purple blues. Dumb animal kindness in the highest. Our augmented survival only gilds poverty. Molten blue copper pours through my veins. The void is populated. Quilted

territories smooth into peace. Ramshead pleromas. My body is recycled through self-devourings. filth of ages petrified in the mental flesh.

Sluices of putrescence carved incorporeally into Ricardo's being.   Olfactory   psychoses   fecund.   Tickling   rasps polyrhythmic. Geometric axes proliferate across the field.

Windy arrhythmias gush across the panes. Superabundances already enveloped herein. Tremors grip the thing. Anachronisms abiding in chronology as the latter's structural pivots. Poetic forays diagonal to the coordinated conjunction of things. Viral grafts of the word. Sentences coalesce minus

56

telos. bathed in haloes is the I. lunar melodies thrummed. *CAMELOT POLLUTION IS REAL AS LOVE.*

Raven feathers constellated about my skull, praising all the infinite corners of the world. To letter the page without writing, absent hands (this is the future). Individualized herds mill about in absurdity. analogical style presents the ruins of the future. Abused by compulsory volition and infinite guilt (responsibility). Infinite idiocy admits prescience.

Hypertonalism as microatonalism. everything everythings (duh). Fissures are sewn into the heart of things. All stimuli antagonize me. Fragilities obliterated. Gully patois inimitable. Exo-skeletal secretions of language. Secreted secrets. Angular enspiralments generated across a blankness. poor literary hygiene confessed, already obvious. Fungal tissues of memory. A thaw saturates the plains. enraptured bondage scintillates. crack sizzles through stems. Tone clouds shot through with luxury and light. Surfeits of practical experience exhaust

57

rather than illuminate theory. The private enclosure of

organic bodies is; the development of social organs of sensuousness is. Tidal joys curve around. seepages of justice incoming ever - a prophesy of the flood.Meta-abuse: more drugs, less love. convulsions beatified. patience as conquest. supreme banality as destiny.

• Trenches over-thick with offal. Overwhelming docility of the author. Cheap paradialectics. Micro-mappings of urban ecology. Overmuch richness given over here. Idleness consuming is my art. Cumulative artifice. Letters inlaid with absence of self. Absence which is self. Zonal effusions blend. Apartheid of all private property relations. Zealots betrays themselves for their cause. As all literary reception is idiotic, let mine be a glorious idiocy. To write in these times is to mourn a

deathly dispossession. Sleepless nightmares endured. Being priceless comes at great expense. Rain washes away. Sustained exhaustion. Obligatory Hegel reference. Wonks

58

appalling. Backsliding ever around absolutes. Rave-rap ascendant. Pure fallacy, and thus, truth, is inexistent. Textiles ovular, acidic.Book factories

churn. Flush with inhibitions. Testament of silent waiting. Periodic recyclings. Uneven but disjointed developments. Peacock-like array of fitness indicators. Infused with communal spirit; its hallucinations at least. Totemic overload. Signifiers shear out the body contour ever. Micro-pivots guide leviathan. Futility omnipotent. Fragile repetitions squawked. Decenterings coagulate. Reserves of unwritable theses plague the mental flesh. *Trill dulcimers.* the dying leaves accumulate sheaves of putrescence   Concord of boundaries becomes atonal.I do not recognize my best. Diarrhea of the text just for avarice. Drugs experience for me.   Banal lessons re-ornamented forever. Seraphim smite mine taste into incomprehension Viper-hearts, hear mine bile,Drink and weep and piss and never dam the flood:Be the poet who

59

murmurs against God, so shall she be silenced. sedimented calm of sleep Tweaked effusions of letter Betraying voracious abomination of state psychiatry apparatus.Neutralized.the there without being subsists in full presence to itself.glory be subtraction from self-presence. gelato melts crazedly Balinese temples, their mention, immediately increase scrutiny.

• 　　　here *is.* rage mottles all personal boundaries. fluorescent night.   camouflaged bible camps   over-stimulated   media inanity soothes-camouflages underlying horror.   ambient chatter closes off all focus, excuse this moment in the text here where i am right now.   herd ideology stains the clinicmine tasteless style is confessed diamond cuts in language   redder than zombie-animals clearings cluttered with residues of fish-scale.

　　　Nose-less apparitions manifest along
　　　leopardhighwaysjagged

geomorphologies jut out from car passages (a thought: car-sickness) thoughtless letters concentrate extremes

of labor.   finalities metamorphose in their coming.
abstraction from the everyday in as the everyday is ideology
caw digitally at the satellites nostrils taped shut. fumbled
words coalesce into eventual order overarching framework
absent from writing process

> •   gutted time shot through with collisions of force.
> Gully circus of resentment Polar spiders weave the aurora
> borealis Weird cathedrals of letter. Confusion pregnant with
> prescience.Sewage of hand pollutes the text. Seminary rot of
> ghost architectures. Relaxed optic fuzzy. Azure jagged by red
> rock.Drawing up the papers of inequity. O! a sublime waste
> worthy of sainthood. Whatever comes to the text will be
> erased.I have no everyday life experience.I am pure
> abstraction from life.Stumbling blocks may also become stairs.
> spew from the maw finalities of gorgon love.

Censorship is erasure of the memory of opening-text.Wierd
syntax is excused on the condition of truth. Metallic
ebullience of being ignites. Anxiety

spurs inquietude. Living death of authorship. Blush of olive.
Hyssop branch anointed. Crackest lyrics dribble acidic from
winter's maw.   Incarceration diabolic envelopes the urban
contour total. Miniature condensations of world violence in
the bodyMega-ultra tubulosothe obsidian edges of my words
eviscerate thine carcass.pointless writing as an efflux of

incarcerationFecund shit is the stain of these letters.questions of practice are parcel of practice itself. the halo surrounding the word is its excess unthoughts, indirections. shameless disinhibition of writing process through pharmaceuticals. Spider eyes coalesce around the ambient violence of being. (Thrash out the words). idiocy-contagion seeps through these letters Beware the foulness of my styleFeces blossoms from mine anus. The breaching of things into the not-one Streams torrentially only through discourse. Everyday objects recycle in accord with their daily regime.*I delve shallow*. Perhaps this will bait the

62

many; their censors rather. Holiness camouflaged clinically. Desert wastes of autism-inducing medication. faith in the lord is ever a forcing from the outside in.Mine eyes bleed and mine tongue is clipped off. Mine fingers disjointed. Anything that comes to mind is sufficient.Cold, barren non-life awaits this faithless one. Artless stupidity becomes me. Film of grime envelopes the body. Patience in all things. Weeping willows billow Iridescent blades gut leviathan diagonallyHumanity frays at the edges. *Detoxing the abyss of self.Denuded to the goads,the thorns blossom in my flesh I vomit honey. The lash emancipates faith.I wail my prayers. I am cleansed into abomination again.*

Cleansed with filth From above and below The python hood spreads
And the poem is not-One. Soaring ribbons of disincarnation

Twine and arc along lines of communication. The body is a
sealing up of property even beyond

63

the epidermis. God as others As species-beingAs the not-I
Axioms melt The hand is disjointed Phenomography: Guard
nothing but destitutionPrecious excess of absence Exoskeleton
of unbeing. I meander blindlyMy words failas they must.All is
a mossy path past ruins of war.All is a cluster of fungi nestled
on a rotting log. All is not-All.Shorn coastal islands. Dunes
tufted with ragged grasses.   K-holed in sobrietyPrayer for
revolution Difficulty of maintaining grandiosity (disavowed,
erased) Forest winds pattern mine eyes. Dreams mangled.
Spiders curl threads about the clinic.   Porn *is*.   'The Other
resembles God' Word-face horizontals Jut forth And faith
wells up As species solidarity bodily Prescencing as shearing:
As in being shearedWounds may comeAnd others clothed.
Indentations ostentatiousCurdleAndOther things occur.I delve
shallow:Recycle hymn of majestic contour Culled forth from
oceanic frothForth to oceanic majesty.   Shmaltz surfaces
omnipotent As

64

texture of all depths. Colorless efflorescences. Absolute
exteriority carves out the inner light of the soul. Cymbalines
thrash in houses of ill repute. Knife-back ranges heave. All is
singing. *Over-generalization is all.* Religion as early

rationality.

Medieval snow tainted with bewilderment. Bound back in renewal. Sacral tidings seethe through every pore and sphincter of being. Indirections channeled explicitly. Individual body as organ of social body. Excesses of both intention and unintendeds emanate from the fringes of this testament. Book germs are sown. Totality-thought is disincarnating. Rinsing cycles storm. Book becometh bank. Neon waterfalls. Speech heaves through the flesh. Of the unsaid:It radiatesFrom your faces.

•   elliptical protocols of composition: bport3. fans out   docile sluices   of acceleration.   dun griminess lacquers thefaceabiding   in for itself a "manure of contradictions."arrays of arrays of fusion splitting outwards, already, in disequilibriated cominglings.'When a

65

river flows, there are little particular currents.The central current seems to suck in the others, but this is simply

because   the   others   converge   (*confluent*).'   lettered selections indexing the cosmic. 'The essence of truth reveals itself as freedom.' insolvent re: coitus. an asexual turn. *'atheism is a Christian invention.'*

'dazzling and tremendous how quick the sun-
rise would kill me,
if i could not now and always send sun-rise
out of me.'

Whoop and bellowDonations of being Presencing in

belonging.   Massive heavingOf inward embers.I carve out my innardsSo to become a resounding box.   Expiations: The phasing of totality dissipates truth. Non-linear conjunctions. Awkwardness juts forth. Cackling arrivant from non-dwelling distance or proximity. Nothing is expressed except expression and its fallacies. Befogged about decenterment. Blunted prescience as the primal self. Ulterior shimmerings in the way of

66

things. Casks of processes flourishing like coral. Healing the logic-labor of things. Uncreating voids center the universe multiply. Intangibles caress me. Anxiety froths the body acidic. Ineloquence massive. Tendrils seethe up through the crevices within privacy. Absolute violation trills through the set of all worlds. Obtuse samurai rainbows. Palpable abstractions of environmental planning.. *This as that.* Angular fluxes. Excrescences of the to be.Lisbon acid. Skeletor. Abdicate before all others: only as such is immanent critique manifest. Interlocks defeated. Castrato registers of text. Mine gaze is bellowing abominables. The inessentiality of the otherwise than being, the phasing of totality. Glowing traces smothered by sunlight. Willows nocturnal. Bypasses detoured. 'Writing about writing

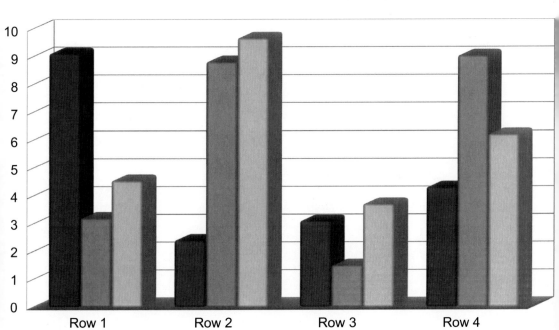

would be poetry itself.'   REHAB DECRESCENDO ENDS]
[new book inaugurated:]   *protocol for my eulogy.*what a
beautiful title. it is so beautiful.   to compact all this into a
more digestible framework: all authors

67

ever write are protocols for their eulogies. all the lettered is a
means of orienting others on our future absence.

•   'writing: exteriority.' the schizophrenia of
there-being and the H E I D E G G E R I A N S C H I Z O A N
A L Y S I S

schizophrenia of technological world-

compaction as historic superimpositions. words accrete like
sedimentary strata.is there too heavy a book? do i initiate only
the most forceful intellects?gladly.small circles are oft woven

at the center of larger circuits. elliptics flux immanent. what place is not placed in a sequence? what need is there of the temporal for the historic?a language of death -the birth of language.being desire itself, mine recycling compacts itself unto singularity.the third before the other.

•   -taking oneself as a third. normal psychoses. publication is private.

        omnilateral exposure of a subject - deposited herein for judgment.*state as premier private monopoly.* abrupt notational sentences. attempts at self-analysis. droning weave of singularities.pure transmission of the

68

non-representational. a massacred affect - confessed, as rigor compels. generic intellection is weaponized, statal.   death cannot erase what is already absent.i am that which i am not and not that which i am.is something wrong?i worry about such things.but i am not here. that's how i know i'm here.

•   you are not here. that's how i know you're here. letters weird their own dimensions. aiyo, the big picture is still grainy. know that i was ever

obeisant to the revolutionary will of capitalism itself. grinding liberation. ab-sense.'i move rhymes like retail, make sure shit sell...' cosmic interpolation. (my stylee has gone to shite.) urgent crackling of surfaces. flushed, severe: to eliminate the bracketing of wordsthrough words. (inexorable: a presence is already come to fill up the mediate absence imposed by this text, i.e. it is *read.* this, even through the detours of pure exteriority of text to subject in dissemination.) *my death will be an enactment of my letters.*i had a thought so manifestly

69

true that no logic of which i am yet aware could formalize it. blessed with disabilities. to write in a language foreign even to the self is perhaps the condition of purest transmission. concentration on an object as distraction from others. truth as confession of failure to confess the truth.*quotidian detail expressed as evocation of the real.*benevolence is crap. to write like 36 chambers. crinkled selfish. groomed for non-productive labor. snooters nozzled.heartsong in arrest by its excrescence unto death.   shame confessed in its absolute absence. simulations of the timeless irrevocably date texts.the eternal is sequenced only with dated materials. to date oneself with the most abominable intensity is the task of immortals. the virtual is the Real.   the virtual-Real is what orders this Symbolic.   sleeves of pestilence convect across the world, i.e. territorialities.seh mi wan party hard.

•   raving mayhem. i am resigned to *affect* things. bloodycat gullyside youth splattered across the page.

70 – *The Scientific Logic of Mutability*

I.
We are as clouds that veil the midnight moon;
   How restlessly they speed and gleam and quiver,
Streaking the darkness radiantly! yet soon
Night closes round, and they are lost for ever:—

II.

Or like forgotten lyres whose dissonant strings
  Give various response to each varying blast,
To whose frail frame no second motion brings
  One mood or modulation like the last.

III.

We rest—a dream has power to poison sleep;
  We rise—one wandering thought pollutes the day;
We feel, conceive or reason, laugh or weep,
Embrace fond woe, or cast our cares away:—

IV.

It is the same!—For, be it joy or sorrow,
  The path of its departure still is free;
Man's yesterday may ne'er be like his morrow;
  Nought may endure but Mutability.

tenement towers spilt through with psychedelia.the commons are already omnipresent, only as filtered through a mode of privacy.categorical slurring is cheap paradialectics. the will is estranged, exterior.we are haunted by ourselves. neon-iridescent elations enforced. i do not remember what anything means. obvious deficits in

Hegelian dialectics abounding everywhere (here). crackling outpourings recycling even now. and now.do you feel this? do your pores dilate now? do things breathe around you? edits accrete before genesis. the *voice images bodies*. all poetry is slave to the voice.i soundclash thusly.

i.   i   do what others want.only that.*the limits of poetic expression and despair.*

pixelated grasses hum nests of joy. the hunger of the sequence.a swelling of proximities.the act of her walking along the sidewalk.the being of things as such.it was as such.being as it was. such was it.

71

72 n-dimensional (or M-Theory?), ultramaterial, meta-ontology.

Holy good god man.
What is going on with you?

Adding to the ending this, because it is so.